M.E.A Lasley

Across America in the Only House on Wheels

M.E.A Lasley

Across America in the Only House on Wheels

ISBN/EAN: 9783337257118

Printed in Europe, USA, Canada, Australia, Japan

Cover: Foto ©Andreas Hilbeck / pixelio.de

More available books at **www.hansebooks.com**

Across America

IN THE

Only House on Wheels;

OR

Lasley's Traveling Palace.

——:o:——

BY

M. E. A LASLEY,

Author of "Sketch from Life's Book of the House on Wheels."

——:o:——

Price. 25 Cents.

——:o:——

House on Wheels Publishing Company,
Room 611 and 612, 150 Nassau Street, New York.

Copyrighted by M. E. A. Lasley, 1899.

INTRODUCTION.

In bringing out this book the author feels it will fill a place untouched by others, the heroes of this book being the only parties that have crossed the American continent in a house on wheels. And having lived in the western country for last twenty-five years, he feels well acquainted with the country, people, resources, climate, etc., and can describe it in more truthful words than those not otherwise posted could do. Experiences of former years are also introduced as touching our present condition and showing causes leading up and preparatory to our successful trip. All figures are accurate or as near as can be procured. This book is of facts, not fanciful sketches. Sketches, pictures, experiences, etc., are from our journal noted at the place and date. This book is not a literary production, but historical and biographical. Read, then judge.

The Author.

Across America in the Only House on Wheels.

CHAPTER I.

A Home Love Scene.

"Say ; Tell me dear, why does there seem to be no mirth in you for the last few days? Have I done or said anything at which you could have felt hurt? You have tried to be cheerful, but I can see that there is something weighing upon your mind. Come, love, tell me, let me know all. Now while 'tis wet and disagreeable outside, come and sit down in the arm chair before the big fire, and while I do some mending tell me what causes you to look sad, even when you smile."

The chair placed, the mother and loving wife in listening attitude, the father began :

"Well, I've been studying our condition over and over, and at last have come to the conclusion that I must leave you."

At this time the two little girls who had been playing in the adjoining room burst into the sitting room just in time to hear their father say that he must leave. It surprised them, and they broke into a plaintive cry: "Oh, papa, dear papa, don't leave us; don't leave your loving family!"

The father's heart was touched at this unexpected display of tenderness, and he caught his little girls in his arms and kissed them. The baby boy, asleep upon the bed, was awakened by their childish cries, and he, too, joined in, letting go one of those cries that only a baby knows how to, and soon he had the attention of the household. The father seeing he was the cause of all this commotion, concluded to change the programme. He grabbed little Robert in his arms and danced around the room, catching the girls in turns—around they go! The mother joined in song and soon the house resounded with love and merriment, lasting until bedtime, when after kissing papa and mama good-night they are soon snugged in their little beds.

"Now, mama dear, sit close by me and I will tell you more. Now dear, you know that I have worked hard and undergone many hardships to make a home for my loving family, and now we are about to lose all, and not being strong I feel sad; so, love, I give you my determination. I'll make a cart and go down into California, earn some money and then send for my darling wife and loving children."

"No, dear; I don't approve of your plan. Tomorrow I will give you a plan I know will succeed. Good night."

The above and much more was a scene that transpired in a little cottage home of an humble, honest mechanic in the frontier town of Port Angeles, on the Straits of San Juan de Fuca, in the State of Washington, late in the fall (November) of 1893.

A Wonderful Woman.—A restful night spent and breakfast over, the active brain of the little wife sought to unfold a plan, the success of which has been beyond the measure of what was anticipated.

"Now, love, listen to me. I will never consent to you going alone. I married *you* to live *with you* not *away from you*. Of course I know 'tis best to leave this wet country. You do as I plan, and all can go together. Build a house on wheels; get another house; wait till spring opens, then we can all go together."

"Build a house!" echoed the husband, after the plan had entered his surprised brain, "I can't; I've no money to buy a horse, and no money to live on this winter."

The loving, determined wife insisted upon the adoption of her plan, and finally the husband, desiring to do the best thing, consented, and the details of her plan were talked over.

"You go down to Dungeness (a farming place) and work this winter, and take your pay in a horse. I will support the family by taking in washing. After getting another horse [we had one] then you follow my plan and build the *house*—the details I will give when you get the team."

CHAPTER II.

Tried and Found True.

"Hello, Mr. Rauchman, do you want a hand?"
"No."
"Do you know who does?"
"No, I don't."
"Its getting dark."
"Yes."
"Looks like it is going to rain."
"Guess it will or 'twill be a long dry spell."

"Why don't you come to the point?"

"Don't see any point to come to."

"Why don't you ask me to alight?"

"You can't smoke here; haven't got my barns insured."

"Plague take it!"

"Take what. Who did you speak to?" and the excited rancher looked around, expecting to find a hobo near by.

"My friend, I am trying to get you to ask me to stay all night."

"Stranger, anything worth having is worth asking for; but you may stay over night if you can eat our hash and sleep with our hired man. You can put your pony in the shed; you will find oats in the bin and hay in the mow; find a trough and get the feed—help yourself; then come into the house."

"Draw a chair up to the fire; you must be damp and cold."

"Yes."

Supper soon being ready, an invitation to partake was accepted—cold boiled pork, boiled potatoes, corn bread, cold biscuits, sauce, preserves, coffee, tea, bread and butter. Supper over, my host says:

"I say, stranger, can you read the papers?"

"Yes."

"Well, I am a populist; will you read the new copy to me?"

"Yes" (Paper all read).

"I say, stranger, let me sell you a horse—got one more than I need."

"Can't buy; I have no money."

"Are you willing to work for one if you can get it cheap?"

"Yes, you bet I am."

"You can do rough carpenter work, I suppose?"

"Yes."

"Well, now listen. My name is J. P. Anderson. I am a Swede. I am a leading farmer in this valley. I desire things not owned by my neighbors. I want a horse power like we used in Sweden. If you can make me one I will give you the horse. See?"

"Yes."

"I'll board you. I'll make a sketch of it, then you make the power. O. K. See now."

After several experimental cuts and tries a wooden horse-power was declared satisfactory; attachment made to cutter; oats, straw and hay cut up nicely. Anderson was very proud of his success, and handing me the halter to the horse, saying, "Now we are both satisfied. I have a new machine; you have a pair of horses [a team]. Good by," This was on December 20th, 1893.

My loving wife was not surprised when I came home with two horses instead of one.

"I knew you would succeed if you would only try. My plan, you see, will be a success."

CHAPTER III.

A Western Wonder.

Now for our *house on wheels.* " Build it same as if it was to remain stationary, sills, floor, walls, windows, doors, canvas roof, side boarded up and down."

My wife said: " I desire to assist you in building our house as much as I can." So we took the cross-cut saw (a seven-foot one), ax, wedges and frowe. We chose a nice white cedar tree. I notched it; then together we used the saw. In about an hour the monster of the forest lay at our feet. Discarding some thirty feet of the lower portion we got to the straight-grained part, cut out a portion, split it up, used the frowe and shortly had shakes (split cedar boards) for the sides and floor. The sills are of red fir.

During the balance of the winter, and between jobs of mattress making and repairing, of which I did all I could get to do, and after serving twenty-two days as a petty juror during that term of court, I succeeded in making a sure enough house, small but comfortable, 14 feet long, 6 feet high, 5 feet wide, three small windows, door in two parts, closing independently of each other; roof heavy duck; under part of roof and inside of the house lined with cloth, then nicely papered.

Now came the tug how to couple it, so as to draw, knowing all other vehicles on uneven ground were subject to twists, and as this was nailed together could not stand twists, for three long days I studied over a new coupling. Finally the idea came, and a blacksmith was instructed to make the coupling of the best iron; we put it on and completely attached the front axle to fore part of the house; the hind axle we morticed into under part of the 2 x 4 fir sills. Not having any springs, no fifth wheel, no bolster on front axle, I placed the large wheels before and the small wheels behind. This plan made it easier to get in and out.

Inside Fittings.

"Now dear, you plan for inside arrangements."

"A sheet iron stove in the corner, just inside the door in rear on right hand side, then a cupboard for my cooking utensils. A spring slat mattress on hinges on wall on right hand side, extending to front; on left hand side a cupboard or locker for dishes and provisions. Then a folding table on hinges; above this pockets for drugs, packages, spoons, knives and forks, bottles, etc. Under the table a box for tools—saws, hammers, wrenches, braces and bits, files, nails, bolts, nuts, tacks, screws, etc. In corner, a commode. In front end a large box for clothing, extra bedding, books and sundries. A high chair for the baby boy and a rocking chair [for the wonderful, enduring wife]."

"Being all completed on the 21st March, 1891, we moved into this *only house on wheels*, sleeping in it to see how it would seem. Neighbors called upon us. We had a social greeting. They christened our home on wheels, "Lasley's Traveling Palace."

On March 22nd we finished putting in place our clothing, medicine, tools, sewing machine, grub (provisions), fastened pictures upon the walls, sold off everything not needed upon our trip, converting it into a little money.

The inside arrangements of our traveling palace should be seen to be properly understood, being the most complete traveling outfit ever constructed for camping.

The Poor Man's Home.

They say that mine is an humble home,
    And they call us very poor;
Yet are the prints of the fairies' feet
    All over my sand floor;
And I hear sweet sounds of mirthfulness
    That greet me at break of day;
And the fairies bright come across my path
    Ere I start with my house away—

And when at eve I am safely camped,
    One fairy will slice my bread,
And little ones will climb my knee
    For a kiss ere they go to bed.
Then let them prate of their houses rich,
    Of their jewels and silver and gold;
I have what is better—fairies bright
    Whose love is not to be told.

The Start.—Everything being in readiness, friends gathered and shook our hands and wished us "good by" for the last time. The horses were given the word "go," and into the street (Fifth Street) rolled our now famous Western Wonder at two o'clock on Thursday, March 22, 1894.

News Clip Condensed.—"Lasley says he is going in his house on wheels to California, but we know he can't get there. He is a rustler, but at a job now he can't do."—*Port Angeles Washington Tribune*, March 20, 1894.

CHAPTER IV.

Camp Life.

"Whoa, there!" ('Tis growing dark.) "Viola, please unhitch the horses; Leona, you take care of baby Robert; I will gather wood for the fire and get water. I will water the horses and feed them. Mama will prepare supper."

Stabling for our horses was found in a vacant barn of an absent farmer, and plenty of good hay given them, which they relished. The stable found was half a mile from our palace, in which the wife and children were camped by the road side in the forest. The woods were very dense; many of the trees were 300 to 400 feet high and the underbrush so thick that a deer twenty yards away could not be seen, although heard, in daylight. Wolves, cougars, panthers and bears being seen by the ranchmen any day along the creeks. The creeks abound with fish that they come to get.

"Papa! papa!"

"What, dear?"

"Oh, I only wanted to know if you were coming. 'Tis so lonesome here in the woods without you," answered the light-haired girl of five summers.

"Come in to tea dear; I have been waiting for a long time! Quite a ways to a stable, is it?"

"Yes, and slow work in the dark. But we are O.K. now."

With good relish we gathered around, and with thankful hearts partook of delicacies obtained from forest, field, water and homes, such as the seasons produce. Small game of all kinds we feasted on at times, I killing it with my revolver (the Western man's weapon) being a good shot with it. Sleeping apartments arranged for the night. The journal was written up by the father. Family devotion over we prepared for and retired to rest. Honest toil bringing the sweetest rest. Washington woods have a death-like stillness, not even the hooting of the owl nor the cooing of the dove breaks their quietude.

An Ever Wakeful Eye.—A year before starting on this trip a neighbor gave us a worthless black run-about dog, saying, "If you can keep him you may have him." Seeing the dog was young and of a good breed, I took him home and commenced training him, fed him well and cared for him. He took well to us, developing fine traits as a shepherd dog. A better hunting dog or a sharper watch dog one needs not want. He has proven valuable to us on this trip. He loves the children, permitting no animal to come near any of them. He won't ride in the house unless compelled to. He is the only animal that has walked entirely across the continent; he traveled every day about twice as far as we did, so he has quite 13,000 miles to his credit. I keep his feet in good condition so that he does not get lame. He is fat and sleek, admired by all lovers of that faithful friend, the dog. He is very intelligent and much loved by us. Nothing troubles camp that he does not know of.

Slow Progress.—*March 23.*—Having called a halt down upon a creek (Morse Creek) of course we had a hill to climb to get up out of the valley. Roads in extreme western Washington are upon high lands, as the bottoms are generally wet and marshy. Oh, what a hill! Steep, wet, muddy, nearly a mile long. Horses were only able to draw the house a few steps at a time; all had to walk; wife had to carry the baby boy, except when I carried him a little way ahead, then resting until we got the team with house up to them. The road was only wide enough for our wagon, except at certain places where teams could pass freely. The timber and brush grow to the very edge of the road, and was so dense that we could not see into it ten feet. abounding with bear and cougar (mountain lion). It was not pleasant to be very widely separated, even on a bright day. The roads were bad (hub deep in places) and rough, and our first hill experience was repeated several times the same day. The road was so bad that at noon we only had five miles to our credit.

Coming to the first ranch (farm) we were hailed by the owner, Charles Agnew. Said he: " Where are you going? Where did you start from? How long have you been on the road? How many are there of you? Say, send the little girl over; got a lot of eggs you can have. Here are potatoes in this pit; help yourself."

The child returned with a basket of eggs and a loaf of bread.

And he added: " Put up your horses in the

stable; feed them oats and chop; just help yourself."

Dinner over, we thanked him, and he insisted that we stay all night, but receiving his blessing, we started forward.

While hitching up the team three ladies and a man came from an adjoining ranch to see us, being the first visitors on the trip. Since then we have had more than a million (1,000,000) visitors.

On arriving at the next ranch (Hoffman's) through the mud, they persuaded us to stop with them over night, which we did. And oh, what an abundance of good grub and lots of horse feed! They tried to get us to sleep in their house but failed; we slept in our palace. We accepted their invitation to *eat* in their house. We had been all day at hard travel and only eight miles to our credit for the day; team and selves tired.

A Surprise at Breakfast.—" I say, Lasley, you had a mattress factory in Angeles, had you not."

" Yes."

" I have a fine mattress that needs overhauling; what is to hinder you upholstering it for me today ? "

"O.K. Just what I'll do. I have **with me** all the requisites to repair with."

At three o'clock the job was finished, and we again hitched up and were ready to start when Mrs. Hoffman said: "You have forgotten something." I went into the house to get it and she handed me $3.00, the factory price for doing the job. I offered to pay for our meals and the feed, but Mrs. Hoffman said, "we do not take pay for accommodation offered." The money we thankfully received, work being scarce.

Again Among Friends.—Leaving Hoffman's with best wishes we pushed forward to Dungeness bottom. We hailed the same ranchman we got the horse of; he recognized us and invited us to stop with them over the Sabbath, which we gladly did. Going to church on Sunday we met many old and dear friends.

At the Metropolis.—At Dungeness we learned that we could go no further, there being no open road, so we decided to ship by boat. The beach is flat at this point; deep water is reached by a dock (wharf) 1,100 feet long. At this place is the mouth of the Dungeness River. When the tide is out a person can wade across the river as it spreads out over the bar; when the tide is in it will swim a horse any place under the wharf.

And oh, the salmon! I saw a net drawn at this point, and it contained 2,200 salmon! For more about fishing see chapter on salmon.

The steamship *Monticello* coming into port I asked the captain to take us to Seattle. "Yes." "How much?" "$20.00," "Only have $18.00 all told, must live, you know." "I will for $15.00." "I'll give you $10.00." "I'll take you for $12.00." "O.K.," said I. Arrived at Seattle at 2 a.m.; on board till 7 o'clock, getting stock and house off on high tide.

The papers heard of us being at the dock: reporters interviewed us; the following is a condensed clipping:

Traveling in Pioneer Style.—A FAMILY STARTS IN A PRAIRIE SCHOONER FOR A SUNNIER CLIME.—A rig more resembling a "prairie schooner" than anything else started from city dock yesterday afternoon on a long journey southward. The occupants were a wife and three children, while the husband, M. E. A. Lasley, of Port Angeles, rode in front and drove the team of horses.

Mr. Lasley has been living with his family in Port Angeles for several years, where he has some real estate.

He said yesterday that he had started for some country where the sun shone more than it did here; he formerly lived in Colorado. The schooner was brought up on the *Monticello* Tuesday and is a unique outfit. It is nothing more nor less than a small *house on wheels.* Mr. Lasley constructed of cedar a very light but comfortable house, canvas roof, three windows, door like a hack. The interior is supplied with all the comforts of an ordinary home for the family on their journey. Lasley carries tools for repairing the house, mending the wheels, shoeing the horses, etc., and proposes to do his own work. His wife was much more anxious to start than he.—*Seattle Post Inteligencer*, March 28, 1894.

CHAPTER V.

Our Family Autobiography.

It may be of interest to the reader to know something of our former history; it will give some idea of the preparations we have had to accomplish such a trip. I will now give a condensed history of

The Queen of the Traveling Palace.—MRS. LASLEY.—She was born about August 25th, 1866, in Greensburg, West Moreland Co., Pa. She was taken to Missouri when very young, then to Iowa, where she was left in the care of a very cruel family near Des Moines. She was beaten by the woman, knocked down, kicked and cuffed, lifted by the hair and ears, caused to stay out-doors with the thermometer below freezing; slept in the stable, poorly fed, bed a pile of dirty clothes while the family slept on the finest feathers; today she bears marks upon her person showing the abuse passed through. The woman's husband was a Dunkard preacher; but his lips were sealed, his life was not his own. Many a time he has slipped a crust of bread or a piece of meat into his napkin to give to poor Mary, who stood weeping outside the kitchen door. Finally the treatment was so hard she ran off to one of the neighbors, barefooted in the snow. They sheltered the broken-hearted girl; sent word to her folks in Colorado, to whom she was sent. Prior to nine years of age she spoke Dutch entirely; but the woman, Mrs. B., whipped the Dutch all out of her, until at 12 she did not know a word of it.

In Colorado she had a checkered life, working sometimes out and at others at her folks; when out at work variety was her lot—some places good, others not. Her home life was never what a home should have been; her wages were never her own, others were benefited thereby. She tried hard and succeeded in her studies, both in school and out, and by dint of diligent application and energy succeeded in getting a good common sense education. Her maiden name was Mary L. Ambrust.

We have learned indirectly that she has property coming to her, but it has been so covered up that she has not yet received her heritage. We get clues to it little at a time and may soon be in a position to force things open.

The Author.—M. E. A. LASLEY was born in Gallipolis, O. My father's folks were Kentucky people; my grandfather was an associate of Daniel Boone. My mother's family were F. F. V's of the Shenandoah Valley, of Virginia. I lived in Gallia Co., O., till I was 19; finished my education in the high school of Denver, Col. Our foreparents fought alongside Gen. Washington; and in the wars of 1812 and 1845, and our parents in the war of 1861. If the reader desires to know more of the writer's history I refer him to our book, **"Pioneer Life in the West, or The Boy from a Buckeye Town,"** being a description of the West from the seventies up to now—range life, cowboy, herder, teamster, mill life, office work, secret service, teacher, athlete, hunter, guide, mechanic, merchant, politician, manufacturer and traveler—showing how a bright intelligent young man can adapt himself to all things in all places, telling what the West really is and what a person must be to succeed well. We can supply you with copies or they can be procured from agents. The book gives several love scenes in which the author took part—as to how I first met the girl that became my wife; where, when and how I wooed and won her; when, where, how and by whom we were married I leave for the other book; suffice it to say that we were married and some two years afterward our oldest child was born. I now introduce to you

Miss Viola E. I., born to us on New Year's day, 1884, in the city of Greeley, Hon. Horace Greeley's temperance colony on Cache-a-la Poudre River in Colorado. Viola is noted for her excellent location, never has been in a city so large as to be any way befogged. She says blindfold her and place her in any part of Buffalo, Cincinatti, Chicago, St. Louis or San Francisco she could easily find her way back to our house on wheels. When only two years and two months old on several occasions she went alone from home down to my shop, distance nine squares (one mile), making turns around three corners. Her education has not been neglected. She does all our marketing and purchasing as a business training. History, biography and travels is her choice reading. Her language is fine. We give both our girls lessons at home. This trip is an educator that can't be excelled. I now introduce to you

Leona Arabelle.—Born to us Oct. 27th, 1888, in Pocatello, Idaho. On a lonely desert sandy plain the town was situated on U. S. land, but the Indians declared it to be on their reservation, and placed the town under Indian police, contrary to the desire of the whites. Many were maltreated, and finally an uprising took place; troops called out; a battle followed; several killed; a new survey was made which demonstrated that the whites were off their reserve. For a description of Idaho reserves, etc., see chapter on Idaho. I now introduce to you our only boy

Robert Mauck.—He was born to us on Feb. 15th, 1893, at Port Angeles, Wash. He was born with a veil. He is a finder of articles lost. Sailors say no vessel will go down with a person on board born with a veil.

During President Lincoln's administration he thought best to prepare a defence for the Puget Sound country, so sent out a commission; surveyed a town; sold off the lots of the present city of Port Angeles, being the first safe harbor on the Straits of Fuca, and the only harbor that sailing vessels can enter in all kinds of weather, and drop anchor without the assistance of a tug. Around this city he left a strip of land wedge-shape, half a mile wide at south end, six miles long and two miles wide at north end and called this Port Angeles town site reserve. Time passed till the summer of 1890, when the residents thought best to get Congress to open this reserve for settlement, so people began to have it surveyed into lots and blocks to correspond to the town, to choose two lots 50 x 140 feet, clear off the lots, of trees, and brush, build houses on their choice and move into them. School-house sites, church sites, society hall sites, grave yards, etc., were chosen and used for purposes designed. Nice residences sprang up as by magic, Where a dense growth of timber grew in a few short months a city of 4,000 inhabitants stood, commanding a fine view of the beautiful harbor (3 x 5 miles, large enough for all our naval vessels to anchor in, if necessary), also a view of the deep green water of the Straits of Fuca. By extending the view the city of Victoria, B. C., is in sight, its electric lights being plainly seen at night. It was upon Port Angeles reserve that our boy Robert was born, on U. S. ground, corner of Fifth and Lincoln Streets. Afterwards titles to these lots were granted us by paying enormous prices to the U. S. for them. On the lot where Robert was born was where we built our Traveling Palace.

Having given you a short acquaintance with our family—they were born under circumstances and in places widely apart—a brief review of us from the time our oldest was born for the next eight years will be interesting.

CHAPTER VI.

True Western Life.

We were running a general mattress and furniture repair shop at the time our oldest was born, and doing financially well. Afterwards we bought a house and lot, were progressing well toward paying for it. A second child was born to us, lived fifteen months, then took sick, got worse, had doctor after doctor for three months, up day and night, no rest; finally the wife took sick, our child died, wife grew worse, my mother assisted me to care for my wife and she got better. Following my wife's improvement mother sickened, grew worse, and at my house, after linging three months on her sick bed, passed away at the advanced age of 75 years. Nursing mother and doing for her my wife, not being strong, got worse. I tended both wife and mother, not knowing which would live longest. After mother died, our physician, with tears in his eyes, said: "Brother Lasley, I feel sorry for you, God knows I do; but brother, to be plain with you, I have lost hope for your wife; poor woman, she is going to die unless—" "Unless what, doctor? You raise hope in my mind by that *unless*; pray tell me unless what?" "Unless you go out camping with her. I have doctored her for ten months now, and medicine will do her no more good. But there is your business; you will lose that." "Business be hanged!" said I, "If I can save my wife and regain her health I will go to any place or do anything for her." He assuring me health would follow, I made preparations for

Our First Camping Out.—Sold my business, made a tent 7 x 7 feet, bought a pony, harness and light wagon, made a wool mattress with waterproof extension cover so that no dampness could reach us from the ground, and when rolled up, folded and tied, covering prevented dust getting into our bed. Got a small camp stove and cooking utensils, provision box and small trunk for clothing; arranged everything to fit into its proper place; put a good cover over our wagon, and with a few dollars in our pocket we started on May 8th, 1888, from Fort Collins, Col., hunting for my wife's health.

The first day she was not able to go far, three miles being all; the next day eight miles, she showing signs of improvement immediately. We put our camp stove on the ground and cooked (I did the work at the start); at evening time we put up our little tent and slept in it. We traveled through the mountains (wife improving rapidly) visiting Salt Lake City and places of interest, fishing, hunting, swimming, etc., till finally on August 28th we landed at Pocatello, Idaho, the place where Leona was born, distance 1,100 miles. When the Indians made war upon us we sold out everything, took the cars and went to Washington (wife in excellent health) it offering inducements to new comers. There I engaged in manufacturing mattresses and repair work. I skip the details of our trip intentionally, for it is one of the interesting chapters of our book, **"Pioneer Life in the West, or The Boy from a Buckeye Town,"** showing how we fared, the scenery passed through, the people met with, how we overcame difficulties in the way, animals that attacked us, fishing, etc., being exciting, pleasing and full of life.

After being in Port Angeles some three years

we concluded to return to Colorado via National Park, sold off personal property, took cars and came east as far Walla Walla, Wash.

CHAPTER VII.
Our Second Camp Life.

Worked on a rancho (all of us walked 30 miles to secure the work) during spring, purchased team, harness and wagon, fitted it up as described in chapter on first camp life, only no tent, slept in wagon instead. Built wagon bed 5 feet wide on hind wheels, 3 feet in front, sheet-iron stove, etc., as before told. On July 5th, 1892, we started eastward. It came on not weather, wife sweltered under the heat (one of the hottest places on a hot day is Eastern Washington), came to a fork in the road, one branch running south east, the other south west; wife called a halt. "I can't stand this heat; let's go back to the Sound country." "O.K., said I, and we turned westward arriving soon in the Cascade Mountain wilds, inhabited by wild animals, toughs, road agents, and bandits. (The detailed account can also be found in our book, **"Pioneer Life in the West."**) Over the roughest road in America we reached Seattle, and then to Port Angeles, Wash., arriving Sept. 3rd,

1892. I again opened a mattress factory. In the winter I was sick several times with fever and general debility. Persons becoming used to the climate there will never leave it and be contented elsewhere. Even now I feel myself longing to return where they have no winter nor summer—same clothing vill do the year round.

CHAPTER VIII.

A New Start.

From Seattle with our only house on wheels. Being again on terra firma, we prepared to go forward expecting better roads; but we were disappointed after leaving the plank road of Seattle. First the house would lunge down into one chuck hole, then into another. Towards evening it began raining; a high hay shed hove in sight; we got permission to drive under it, and stop for the night; feed was procured by asking; comforts of camp soon formed; evening spent with visitors who came to see us, and they let it rain.

Clever Farmers.—Next morning being clear we pushed forward, over worse roads if possible. At evening, by invitation, we drove under the shed of a hop house, again entertained visitors, and we let it rain.

Beautiful day dawn again. Roads somewhat

better. We had been going up White River Valley. Dinner was over. We were approaching the small town of Auburn in high spirits, hoping we might find work to do, our money being low—$3.00. We tried to get work but failed. This place though only 28 miles from Seattle, had taken us three days to cover that distance.

CHAPTER IX.

Clouds O're Cast.

Entering Auburn, a man approached and hailed us. Said he: "I am an officer; your team is attached; you will find them at the livery if you want them." He unhitched them and led them away.

A Trying Hour.—The action of the officer had attracted the attention of the town **loafers, bums, idlers,** etc., who laughed at our misfortunes— "odd house, team," etc, This was too much for my poor wife. She, in agony of despair, broke down, and wept as only a woman can weep when she sees all her hopes crushed. The children, seeing their mother weep, commenced crying also. All this was trying to the husband, he turned, hid his face and wept silent tears, but only for a moment. He turned upon the crowd; "You will please leave; your presence disturbs us." There was something magical in the request; in a moment they were gone. Turning to his wife he said, "Come dear, cheer up; all will be well." She laid her hand confidingly upon his arm, saying, "Right you are, love; I will try for your sake; but Oh, how dark it looks!"

The Cyclone Burst.—Toward evening a burly looking man approached us. "Well Lasley," said he, "I have you in my clutches. You do as I say, and I'll release your team; refuse, and you can return to Seattle 20 days hence and hear my complaint against you. My advice is this; I'll count the interest on the $50.00, add costs, the total I find to be $72.00. You give me your joint note and a mortgage on your Port Angeles house and you may go." (To the devil thought he to himself, as far as I care.) We accepted his *kind* offer, gave the mortgage and **left** the town.

Facts Stated.—Leading up to the foregoing. We filed on 160 acres U. S. land as a pre-emption in Dec. '89 and commenced building a log cabin. The claim was $2\frac{1}{2}$ miles back of Angeles. During January the snow fell deep. On Feb. 16 I took a man (Ed. Armbrust) with me, packed over the snow our tools, grub, blankets, etc., and commenced felling timber, and in a few days had up a cabin 20 x 16 feet, roofed with clapboards, built upon the snow. A fire was built inside this cabin and the process of thawing out this block of snow and ice commenced, and the cabin began to sink. Strange to say, this cabin inclosed the one constructed before the snow fell.

An Interesting Chapter might be written describing how Ambrust and I set fire to a big tree, 8 feet across, burned it down and camped in the trench made by the tree burning; how we endured exposure; how I fared after Ambrust returned to his home, staying alone accompanied by the lonely howl of hungry wild animals, depending upon God and my revolver for protection; how I completed the house for the reception of my family, which I brought out on April 20, 1890, the snow having melted enough to allow a pack horse to be used.

Funny Sketches.—Several times the horse got off the trail and I had to dig him out of the snow. It makes us laugh now to remember the grotesque figures we cut. Our pack horse waded in the snow above his knees, except when he made a misstep, and then, oh, such scrambling, reaching here and there to find the hard path; or the husband, who carried the youngest child upon his back, Indian fashion, would go down with one leg, then see him scr nble! Or the patient, loving wife would have the same experience; sometimes all of us down at one time. Oh, 'tis funny now to think of, but excuse us from further experiences of like character. In Nov. '90, we found a contest filed against us by one Fowler.

Blackmailing Scheme.—The purpose being to compel us to give him 40 acres to withdraw, supposing we had no money to contest with. March 1st, 1891, set for hearing. Not much money in mattresses; by March we were out of cash, but a friend (John Murphy) gave me the money to meet the contest. The office decided I must have a lawyer and recommended one. (He had practised at Washington, D. C., now of Seattle.) He agreed to defend me for $25.00, thinking to get it dismissed, but *if it continued then to carry it through all the courts for $50.00, to receive his pay when I got my title to the land.* The Seattle Land Office decided that my proof should be allowed.

Fowler Appealed to the General Land Office. After two years it was decided in our favor. He then appealed to the Secretary of the Interior. In Dec. 1894 our claim was affirmed. On

August 8th, 1895. I received word at Corinth, Utah, that I had until August 12th, '95, to furnish Seattle Office with $200 to pay for the land; after that date my claim would be cancelled. I asked for an extension of time. Seattle Land Office refused me; I appealed to General Land Commissioner, he refused to extend; I finally appealed to the Secretary of the Interior; he refused to review, so I lost our claim.

CHAPTER X.

New Openings.

Having given an account of how we lost our home and our ranch, will again refer to our trip and pass hurriedly along. Through Puallup Valley; hop fields ready for twiners but ground too soft to walk upon; beautiful rich valley, but no work for us. Tried Tacoma; proprietor mattress factory said he "had laid off 15 hands; no work for few left." We were at Tacoma on April 1st. Oh, the storm we encountered—rain and blow. *Then southward again*, coming to Mt. Ranier, a station on S. P. R. R.; stopped at store to buy feed; remarked "could buy only small amount as money was short." *"Why not go to work?"* "Work;" echoed I; "What at?" "Teaming, *hauling shingles*; more work than can get teams to do; big job all summer." "O. K.; but have no wagon." "I'll loan you wagon. You go over to my ranch for it, only six miles west; can buy hay three miles further west from there." I stopped. Next morning went for wagon and hay; returned, fixed wagon up with rack. Next morning went to the mill, four miles. "Yes, will give you 9c. per 1000 to haul to town and put on cars." Found 9 teams hauling—nothing else for teams to do. The roads! (well, no roads at at all) mud hub deep. Eight thousand shingles made a big load over such roads. Teams in each others way. Some days two loads, some days one, other days none. Finally pay day came; in fact, they were preparing to close down and were shipping all they could before pay day. I got a tip to demand my pay before shingles left the depot. They seemed surprised; I insisted. They parlied; I threatened to attach—they paid me. The next day the manager and foreman took the trainload of shingles to Portland, Or; and failed to return. The mill hands, teamsters and storekeepers attached the timber, shingles (2d class), bolts, etc. The mill was only rented. They ran the mill till bolts were used up; sold the shingles and paid themselves. 1 counted up my profits; I put in 10 days and cleared $6.40 all told. I then had gained experience and was ready for more.

CHAPTER XI.

First Fording.

Six miles southwest from Ranier we came to an obstacle—a river with no bridge, no ferry. We unhitched a horse, mounted to his back and plunged into the turbulent water, swift and muddy, bottom full of holes, some very deep. Finally, after plunging round up and down, decided to try, so quartered house up stream, the water came into the house, but steadily we neared the opposite bank. Other teams approached but turned back, not willing to brave it. We were all thankful when we reached the top of the opposite bank, preparatory to climbing broken hills underlaid with coal and building stone—the best in the West.

We rested over Sunday and enjoyed the hospitality of Western people, (unknown in the East,) being entertained with strains of sweet music, both vocal and instrumental; listened to declamations, etc., ate at their table and had a general fine time. The following days brought no changes, roads in timber bad; on prairie, fine.

CHAPTER XII.

Classified Experience No. I.

Plank road 18 miles. For the last 10 hours we had been in mud knee deep, team tired out, crossed a set of divide hills approaching Cowlitz River, in woods, growing dark, road slumping, all of us tired and weary, when a crash came, a scream of a child, and all was still, except for the sobbing of a woman. The wheel on lower side had broken. The house lay over on its side. With superhuman strength the father liberated the mother and children, unhitched the team, placed bedding and children upon them, went forward three miles and found a barn, fed team hay, and we slept in the mow. The farmer, Wm. Boon (aged 72 years), next morning was surprised to see us, but after explaining the situation to him he treated us very kindly taking the family into his house and fed them. I went back and brought forward the house on skids; he kindly gave me repairs, showed me now to refill the wheel and set the tire, making my first of the kind. I did some mattress work for him, taking flour, bacon, potatoes, lard, beans, onions, dried fruit, coffee and tea for my pay. Resting over Sunday, we were again ready to start forward. With tears in his eyes he bade us good by, and hoped to meet us in heaven. Approaching Cowlitz River the roads improved. At evening we camped upon the grassy bank of that beautiful river. The flat-bottomed boats came up from Portland to several miles above where we were encamped, bringing in merchantable goods, machinery, etc., returning with shingles, hay, hops, corn, potatoes, beef, stock, horses, hogs, sheep, game, lumber, coal. plaster, gypsum, charcoal, pottery clay, molasses, wheat, oats, dried and green fruits, poultry, eggs, butter and cheese. While we were camped there that eve a beautiful steamer hove in sight and soon then a line ashore; stopped and took on a load of hay, wheat and oats for Portland. We asked the captain how much would take us down to Portland. "$20," said he. Not having the $20 concluded not to ship.

Experience No. 2.

Hopes Brightened.—In the morning a farmer (an Irishman) called. Said he: "I can get you work." "O.K.," said I. "Come," said he. So back on the road we went to his ranch, three miles on foot through fields and over hills, took took his boat and crossed the river, then three miles further. The farmer was plowing at a place a mile still further. "Well, Charles, I've brought you a hand, as you told me to." "Am sorry," replied he, "wife's away on a visit, mother's down sick, sister's getting ready to be married, the boys gone fishing. I can't do the cooking so can't take hand now. I need one, sure. Plowing not done, got lots of wood to chop, crops to put in, fences to build, lots of cows to milk, butter to make, etc. Am sorry, Mike, but can't make room just now. In a month or so—shall want one then, sure. Good day." We returned to Mike's ranch at noon. His man Friday had dinner ready. "Let's eat," said he. Dinner over. "Here, take these,"— canned preserves, 5 pounds butter, 2 loaves of bread, raddishes, onions, lettuce, dried fruit and dried corn. "There, your trip shall not be for nothing; if I had more you should have it; success on your journey. Good by." It was growing late in the day when tired I reached our House on Wheels. The farmer where we camped said, "'Tis grown late in the day; stay now till morning." We did.

The Tug of War.—Ready early and forward. Road less used and unworked, the cuts narrow and the holes deep. Arriving in a cosy nook in an open bottom, we came to a fine farm well cultivated, beautiful house, well kept lawns, flowers, etc. Counted 22 hands. Now I'll get work. Found the owner; asked for work. He said: "No. I have more hands than I can use to to advantage. But come here; put this sack of flour on your shoulder, and this side of meat may come handy." "Yes, 'tis a nice place. I have 72 acres of hops, largest single hop farm in the State." Companies own larger, but no one man. This farmer's name was Mr. Paterson.

Three miles below we came to C. P. R. R. station and post office. Old stage station before R. R. came, now wagon road was abandoned over the mountain, not been a team over it in 7 years, washed out, bridges gone, trees down across roads, etc.

Experience No. 3.—A Perilous Ride.

Said ranchman: "You can't go over that way; will have to ship by cars or by boat." "Can't, no money. I'll try the mountain." "You may die trying, but you can't go with that rig. Team balky, a'nt they!" "Yes." "Never can get over. I've lived here 40 years. I know." "*Can't* never did anything; I'll try it." "Well go, you fool; you will soon come back."

Two wood-choppers seeing us determined to

go, said they would go along for company rather than walk the R. R. They carried about 30 pounds of grub; I said, "Put your pack inside, I can haul it." "Thanks." Up, down, up, up, down; over, across, up, up, up, down; up, down, up; cut trees out of way, filled up washes, rolled stones out of way, made temporary trestles, etc., and finally started down Mt. Pomfry. The further the steeper. A wash in the road, shallow and narrow at first grew wider and deeper. One man took the children and walked ahead down the mountain. He said he "dared not look at the house, expected to hear it go tearing down the mountain." The other man walked behind and said he, "I held my breath for fear; at places the washout was 8 feet deep under your house." I rode, held the brake with my foot and talked encouragingly to my team. One misstep or blunder and over we would have gone. Finally we appoached the bottom of the grade, and oh, horrors! *the road had slipped down into the river!* The wash had opened wider. Timber on both sides; nothing to do but make a square turn on the very brink, and it a sidling one. One slide, slip or fall and house, team and self go over the brink 80 feet below!

My voice trembled, the man behind hid to keep from seeing me go over; the man ahead cried, "Stop, don't try!" I held firm to my team, "Steady! s-t-e-a-d-y! s-t-e-a-d-y!" My little loving wife looking around with a cheery voice, cried out, "Oh, you'll make it! Come on! Come on!" and she came back a few steps. The horses seeing her surged and set the house back upon it wheels, it toppled, she ran and threw her weight upon the upper wheels and saved it going over; the point passed, we stopped around the curve. I procured my rope and tied the house to a tree, the wife holding it while I steadied it a few feet further, then danger was passed. A few rods ahead a tree 5 feet across had blown down, leaving trunk hanging on top of stump. The old road went under. I measured the height and found I had a foot more house than room, stone ledge under tree, only way to pass was between tree and bluff, had a foot more bank than width of wheels; fastened wheels to stump and slid house around it, then down again. Finally the bank was too steep; my nerves too tried, so tied rope to back axle of the house and around stump and lowered it; wife steered the front. (See illustration.) One man was down the mountain with children, the other had gone only to appear when the bottom was reached. The plucky wife, Viola and I got the house down as best we could.

Experience No. 4.—A New Enemy.

Reaching the bottom, a stream was to be forded, water 2 feet deep and full of large boulders, but we got cross all right. On trying to ascend the bank our Dungeness horse refused to pull. After trying several times in vain, the banks being so steep, the horse came off his feet and slid backwards into the stream. While trying to get out a runner came down the creek crying, "Look out for the water; the dam is cut!" New energy was put into us; new ideas. The men said, "You're gone!" Again my rope came into play. Tying the rope around the big horse's neck, then up the bank and around a stump, I gave the word, "Try again!" The big horse lunged, I took up the slack, we blocked the wheels. Again a lunge, slack taken, progress slow but sure, continuing till top was reached. We were up and out of the way when the rush of water, logs, brush, stone, and trees came dashing down where we were but a few short minutes before! We were very thankful we escaped.

The Men Left Us.—They had accompanied us to where they were making shingle bolts and cord wood. In our excitement we forgot to learn their names; an exchange of courtesies and we parted. Very tired indeed we were that night. We felt discouraged and down-hearted, knowing what we had gone over, and still being in the mountains did not know what was before us. The next morning opened fine, our courage was renewed and we were ready for

The Battle of the Day.—We encountered a windfall, big timber lay every way, and finally a tree 8 feet thick lay across our road, and lying across others it hemmed us in. Examining it, we found that by cutting criss-cross, round through the timber, here a small log, there a small tree, we could get through. This monster lay across our path, but its size had diminished. We were 200 feet from the road, and the tree was only 22 inches through. Taking my ax and saw we cut our way through, and some 3 hours afterward were again on the old road, tired and sore. In the evening we arrived at Sandy Bend, on the Cowlitz River—horses played out, harness broken, grub getting low, money gone.

Work Procured on a hay baler—it was hard and dusty, wages $1.25 and board, took part pay in hay for our team; worked till hay baling was through then looked for other employment. Cash received for baling $8.10.

Young Ferry Woman.—The Cowlitz River is narrow but deep, few regular ferries and far apart, but one place a traveler is sure of getting across day or night, that is at Nelsons across from Sandy Bend. The family is large in number but small in size, the oldest being girls, one a Miss Nelson, is the boatman, she can handle a row boat to perfection, she is of fine form, beautiful to look upon, a fine conversationalist Says she "can swim like a duck, and has saved several persons from drowning." Is an excellent shot with a gun; can drive a team or play an organ; play croquet or be a coquet—is truly a Western girl.

The Columbia was on a bender, and higher and higher it came, cutting off all chance of going forward by flooding the bottoms.

A shingle mill offered me a job at bolt hauling. Having some experience (see Chapter X, page 36) I looked with suspicion upon it. but being the only chance I fitted up and began.

The Old Song.—From May 18 till the 26th, Down the roughest hills, 15 bolts making a cord. I hauled 28 to 36 at load at 75c per cord 2 loads per day, in a week I made $21.25, and demanded my cash. He was surprised. Said he "I have no cash to pay you, provisions only" (at high prices). Being trapped we waited, using horse feed and our grub on the bill. On June 14 decided not to wait longer, demanded a due bill and received it, got the captain of a river steamer to accept it and give us passage, with our outfit, to Portland, Or., and allow us $1.40 extra cash.

Experience No. 5.—A Cyclone.

While killing time waiting, I was reading to my wife, in the shade of a beautiful tree, when suddenly the sky became overcast, darkness came on rapidly, a mighty roar in the distance, then all was still as death. Chickens ran to cover, hogs began to squeel, dogs commenced to howl—a mighty storm was coming down upon us. My wife cried, "Our children!" Said I, "'Tis too late! They're at a neighbor's, half a a mile away. We must seek shelter!" Grabbing up our boy, Robert, wife and I sought shelter in a low log shed against a high bank. The storm broke, blackness prevailed, leaves, dirt, sand, boards and debris flew everywhere; the noise was deafening, the roar of falling timber and crashing houses was terrible to listen to.

When it passed the sight was terrorising to look upon—trees 3 feet across broken like pipe stems and barns destroyed. We were in a protected place; where the storm spent its fury was about 200 feet from us. No one happened to be killed. Our two girls were safe; we were thankful.

High Water and Our Boat Ride.—June is the time the snow causes the Columbia to rise. 1894 saw the highest water ever known there, both river bottoms were covered deep with water and mud. One place on the Columbia the water was over 20 miles across it. Looked queer to us to see barns 60 to 100 feet square fastened with stout hawsers (rope) to great trees to keep them floating away; large brick and stone buildings, you could see only the windows of the stories; frame houses were roped like the barns to keep from straying. We saw one large barn being towed up the Columbia by two big tug boats; it had gone astray about 60 miles.

Arriving in Portland, Or., we were landed on 2d Street—a temporary landing place.

Experience No. 6.—A Sorrowful Sight.

The ridiculous things sometimes amuse; we laugh at the commotion we created upon the streets of Portland. Driving along one of their avenues to pass a team it caused us to get on sideling part, and down went one corner of our house. Quickly dismounting, discovered same wheel broken down as before described at Boone's. A curious crowd gathered to see; my brave little wife could not refrain from tears; broken wheel, among strangers, not cash enough to get wheel repaired, crowds poking fun, etc. Finally she became her composed self again, and we turned to with a will and removed our house to a by-street, began fixing the wheel up, when a fine looking man appeared. Said he "Don't bother yourself about your break-down this evening. I'll call on you at 7 in the morning and we'll see what is the best to do." Also spoke a few kind words to my family.

Saturday June 16, 7 A. M.—We rose early, the stranger came. Said he, "Follow me." I did, telling family "I would be back when I returned." Down streets, round corners, over trestles, arrived at a wheelwright's. Said he, "William; here is a man who has a broken wheel; give him an old one, can't you? Go in," said he, "look over those in that room; if you find one bring it out." I found a good one, brought it, and asked the price. Said he, "My friend tells me your situation. You can have the wheel freely. No thanks at all, you are welcome to it." After showing me how to return, my benefactor departed; both refused to tell me their names. The wheelwright's name I could not get; the other one I learned was a Populist, a Christian, a member of the Methodist Church, and his name W. F. Miller. By noon we were again ready to go forward. Just as we were starting we had

A New Encounter.—An expressman hailed us. Said he, "I am directed to deliver these groceries to you." I said there was a mistake. "No, no!" said he, "Order said 'House on Wheels.' I'm right, they're for you." I said I had not ordered any. "Never mind, they're paid for." We took them thankfully, from whom we never knew, but surmise that this Mr. W. F. Miller knew who paid for them. Flour, bacon, sugar, beans, coffee, tea, cheese, crackers, dried fruits, etc.

Experience No. 7.—Miraculous Escape.

Tuesday, June 19.—From Portland we learned there were two roads south—the hill and the valley. We were misdirected and took the hill road to our sorrow. While traveling the hills, over stones, etc., the children were playing, romping in our house on wheels—a scream! I heard a thud; I suddenly tightened the reins, checked the horses, sprang from my seat. Oh, horrors! My child, Leona, had fallen backwards out of the door (which was then on the left side of the house). There she lay, right before the hind wheel! Taking in the situation at a glance I leaped to her rescue in time to grasp the wheel with one hand and my child with the other, stopping the wheel and drawing my own from sure death! "Thank God!" came involuntarily from our lips. I lifted her in my arms and again mounted my seat. The wheel only bruised the flesh, turning it black. By rubbing her back I removed all the soreness and she was soon herself again.

Experience No. 8.—Our First Audience.

There is one thing that impresses our memory that can't be erased On Wednesday, June 20th, following the main traveled road, we came directly upon the main street of Oregon's capital (Salem). I leaned out and asked for the road to Eugene. I stopped to hear the answer, and ere we could start were captured by people curious to know our history, etc. I bore up under the gaze and questions well; my wife and family closed the door and blinded the windows, refusing to be interviewed. It looked queer to us to see bankers, merchants, brokers and clerks hatless around us, a motley set, indeed. Next day the papers told of our Traveling Palace.

For the Sunny South.—Considerable excitement was caused last week by the appearance on Commercial Street of a house on wheels. The conveyance belonged to Mr. Lasley, who is moving his wife and three children from Port Angeles to Southern California.

The house is perfect, fitted with doors and windows. That it is the most convenient mode of traveling cannot be doubted after a glance inside—stove always up, house plants entwined about, beds and table folded up, as a palace sleeping and dining car. While the husband drives the team, the wife prepares the food within, so that when the halt is made nothing is to be done but raise the table and take the dinner from the stove. It is original with Mrs. Lasley, and is a good pattern for others to copy after.—*Salem Independent*, June 21st, 1884.

Experience No. 9.—A Funeral Averted.—

Saturday, June 23d.—My wife asked to ride along side of me, on the driver's seat. "'Tis narrow, but I would like to try while the roads are level." I said. "Yes." Said she, "Let me drive; you hold our boy." When crossing one of those small culverts placed diagonally across the road (a blessing Oregon has lots of) the house lurched sidewise; throwing my wife off against the nigh horse, and under the fore wheel. In falling she had carried the lines with her, so I had no way of stopping the team. I gave them them the word to stop, the wheel had rolled upon her skirts, pinning her down, passing between her limbs and striking her body. Horses stopped suddenly, but the impetus of the house carried them forward. Their stopping kept my wife from being crushed by the wheel had it run lengthwise over her. (The weight of our outfit was 2,106 pounds.) Seeing the dilemma of my wife I leaped over her prostrate form, forgetting that I had our baby boy upon my lap, and grabbed the fore wheel and lifted it off her. I then lifted her into the house. I had dropped our baby and he lay on the double-tree and cross-bars, not even crying; he was unhurt. Examination showed that wife's shoulder was dislocated and body bruised. The wife in arranging her disheveled hair got her arm in such a position that the shoulder went back into its place and has been all O.K. ever since.

Experience No. 10.—Viola's Close Call.

We had camped upon a grassy spot. Viola in arranging things passed near the horse I had purchased at Dungeness; he lunged at her but his halter tightened in time to save her. He caught her clothing on top of her shoulder and threw her from him, scaring all of us, but doing no harm. I tied him to a tree and thrashed him soundly; never again did he try biting any one.

My First Horse Trade.

Approaching Eugene, at the head of Willamette Valley, a farmer asked me to "trade my 1,600 pound horse for a nine year old 1,000 horse, sound and true?" I said, "Yes, even, by giving me a bag of oats." Next morning he said "I would not trade back for $25." I said, "Glad of it; I also would ask you $35."

CHAPTER XIII.

Mountain Fastness.

After leaving Eugene the mountains approach on the east and west. Passing Cottage Grove the valley is only about half mile wide. A sharp turn in the creek brings you suddenly to the foot of a very long and steep mountain. The general trend of the mountains has been north and south. We have been following the valleys, but now a change in them. Spurs from the Cascade Range extend westward, connecting them with coast range. Across these we must make our way. Our introduction is a surprise to us; we expected to go up then down then up again, etc., higher and higher, but this time no down came, but up, up, higher and higher. These mountains are covered with timber and underbrush, and the settlements are sparse and far apart from the Willamette Valley in Oregon to Sacramento Valley in California). Five hours we climbed; a level cleared spot appeared, also a ranch house, we decided to get our dinner. After feeding our team, hitching up again, the ranchman came out. Said he, "You will need help to get the rest of the way (3 miles), no teams go up alone; you can't, I know." "How much cost?" asked I. "$3.00," said he, "to help to pull you through the mud and up to the top of the mountain with my team." "No thanks," said I, "we will play it alone." "You'll never get up alone; if you come back for me I'll charge you $5.00!" "Adiose!" said I. As we started a large team passed having 200 feet of lumber on a running gear. "This," said the driver, "is a heavy load. (Allowing 4 pounds to the foot makes 800 pounds.) "You can't get up the mountain " He led the way. We followed, family all walked, some places my team could only draw our outfit 10 feet, but they kept trying and going up! Finally, after hard work we arrived at the top. Said he, "I never saw as good pulling team in all my life. I have lived on this mountain for years and never saw as small a team as yours draw as large a load up that mountain. You can go any place on earth you please with that team; this is the worst hill between Seattle and San Francisco!" (Where there is any road at all.) The going down was dry but extra steep and stony.

Experience II.—Haying.

June 28.—Arriving at Wilber, Or., got a job haying at Mr. Short's, for 75c. per day and board. Half day hauling on 29th. Saturday, said he, "Rest today, I am going a fox hunting." I used the day looking for another job; none found. Sunday to church. Monday, July 2, work hauling hay. July 3, again hauling hay. In the evening I asked for cash to buy some provisions. Said he, "I have no cash; will give you an order on the store." "O. K.," said I. He counted up my time. Amount $1.90 for 4 days used and lost. Order presented, shopman said, "I will honor this, but no more. I can't carry him longer." The next day being 4th July the Short family went north to a celebration, 18 miles, leaving hay open in field. We decided that we could not fool around there at that rate so went southward 12 miles. Celebrated by going salmon fishing at Winchester.

Sights of a Life-time.—At the mill dam, around the end of which was left a run for the salmon. Fishermen stood there with their spears, and when a salmon dared to try to run the gauntlet each fisherman tried to catch it. Sometimes a fish succeeded in getting through. The larger fish, not daring to try the run-way, tried the dam. The dam measured ten feet, the water pouring over it about a foot deep. The fish would leave the water below the dam, leap into air. Some few would clear the dam into the water above it; many of them fell into the water and sink out of sight, to renew the leap again, may be to fail, may be to scale it. Salmon never go down stream after once starting up to spawn, until their season is over.

A Money Change.—On arriving at Roseburgh we had 90 cents ; bought material, made composition solder, also soap to remove tan, freckles, etc. My wife said she would sell these articles to ranchmen for something to live upon, rather than have me looking for work where none **was** to be found.

The Oregon ranchmen (farmers) told me but few of them had made enough to pay their taxes for the last 3 or 4 years; could not hire their work done; nothing to pay with. One offered me beans at 5c. per pound in exchange for work at 75c. per day. (Found beans not exchangeable at store for more than 2c. per pound.) "No thanks; I want pay for my work."

My wife, (at her self-imposed task,) found first few ranches no good, but soon potatoes, apples, cherries, turnips, bread, hay and cash appeared in exchange for solder and soap. Our day's travel shortened, but our provisions increased. So did the heat! My wife, sold only to the ranches, skipping all the villages; I canvassed the hotels for upholstering—none found.

Glad Surprise.—One ranch deserves more than a passing notice. On Myrtle Creek my wife approached one, and a middle-aged woman asked, "What do you desire? Are you selling something?" This was spoken in a rather rough voice, not encouraging; but the wife, fearing nothing, commenced her song by apologizing for offering things for sale, mentioned her children also, and said her husband was unable to procure work, etc. Said she, "Yes, I will exchange some fruit, potatoes and a hen for your solder, etc. I also have a couple of lounges I desire repaired; your husband can do the work for me." (This was Friday evening, July 6th.) She ordered our team put up and fed hay and grain. Saturday, worked on lounge. Sunday, neighbors called to see us. By Tuesday evening I had overhauled two lounges—received potatoes, cherries, plums, butter, cheese, feed for our team four days, and $2.00 in cash. This family proved to be a Christian family, the old grandma and all. The worst side first shown improved on acquaintance. On Saturday her son was thrown from a horse and broke his arm. I took pleasure in setting and splintering it. Name, Mrs. Adams, P. O., Myrtle Creek, Or.

Experience No. 12.—Morality vs. Hunger.

Camped at head of Cow Creek Canyon. No feed, no ranch, and dark. Next morning early forward for hay. At foot of hill, three miles, came to ranch and lots of hay; asked to buy some. But he refused to sell. Turning a bend I took advantage of the position and "borrowed" a cock of hay (not repaid it yet); the horses had a good meal.

After breakfast we went forward four miles; met an old man. Said he, "Sir, you are off your road; this goes to R. R. station down the creek; you must cross that range; go back five miles and take left-hand road," so returned to the ranch where I had borrowed the hay; got there just as they were going to dinner. Inquired for the proper road to Grant's Pass. Said they, "You must return the way just come; 6 miles below the road turns to the left across mountain." Again asked to buy hay for our team for noon. Said, "No! I told you this morning I would not sell you any." Again I "borrowed" hay for team's dinner, and fed at the same place we breakfasted.

CHAPTER XIV.

Experience No. 13.—Robert's Tussle with Death.

Arriving in Ashland, Or., July 14th. Fine offers for business were held out to induce us to stop. Believing advice good we did. On 18th July rented shop and tried for work—*poor success.* A few days later our boy took summer complaint, and for three months we carried him on a pillow, expecting death every hour, but determined to save him if nursing would do it. Finally, a change; he commenced to get stronger; as soon as the little one was able to ride we decided to start south again en route to Southern California.

During our stay I decided to remodel the

House on Wheels. I took it to pieces, shortened it 2½ feet, placed door in rear instead of the side, opened the front so as to sit inside. Curtains closed it when not in use.

On Nov. 10 we again hitched up. Cleared in cash $5.00 in four months in Ashland. All of us were in high glee to be on the road again, away from sickly Ashland.

CHAPTER XV.
Experience 14.—Hard Road to Travel.

Twelve miles from Ashland, up Sisque Mountains, arrived at a toll gate over a road that a person should be paid to travel over instead of paying. We parlied over the price of gate fee (a dollar). Finally, he looked into our house. Said he, "I'll take that fine high chair, allow you $1.50." (For the $2.50 chair.) So he got our boy's chair for toll! Then up to the summit then down into a river valley. High and cold.

Mount Shasta.—That famous mountain is in sight for miles, towering thousands of feet above any of its neighbors. The crater of the old volcano is grand to look upon. It stands second in height on the Pacific (in the U. S). Mt. Ranier, near Tacoma, Wash., is the highest. Either of these are majestic to look upon, and grand to go upon. Came to Sacramento Canyon at Densmore. We tried to buy hay and grain; none in town. Said they, "3 miles below you can buy both hay and grain." Forward, but no ranch. We had a few pounds of grain left, so tied up our stock to trees (sheep had cleaned up the country of grass). Day's travel 25 miles. The scenery grand and beautiful. Sometimes our road was down upon the roaring, foaming, surging Sacramento River; other times, 2,000 feet above the river. The mountains still above us. The mighty river could be plainly seen foaming and lashing, but not a sound reached our ears. The roadway, blasted out of the side of the mountain, is just wide enough for one team, except in places, where it is widened to let teams pass. After passing one of these wide places teamsters have to "hello" to let approaching teams know their location. The first giving the alarm is entitled to the right of way. Approaching Shasta we overtook a team. We camped together at the head of this canyon. I said, "Bacon, you go ahead; if you break down then I can help you repair. I can keep up with you easier than you with us." He had to do the hallooing, and by allowing him to be about half a mile ahead he stopped any team from meeting us."

Once in this canyon, no outlet till you get through, 80 miles in length. It is the longest passable canyon in the U. S. Road crooked, in some places stony and rough, in other places good. The canyon must be seen to be understood. Back on the higher mountains I was told hunting was good, deer abounded. Second day, distance 25 miles; third day, 30 miles; good roads, plenty grass at night in a field.

Uncle Sam's Salmon.

We will now inspect a salmon hatchery at Pitt River, Cal. A long row of buildings; a dam and gates kept large salmon from going up further. Officers caught them in large nets, sorted them according to size, shape, color and sex; put them in water boxes, and millions of eggs were taken from the females. After milking the males, all the salmon were then thrown back into the river. Down the stream they went, the season's journey up was over. After the eggs are hatched, the small salmon are sent to different streams and rivers to restock them, thereby keeping up the supply that would soon become exhausted if not for the part taken by our Government.

Salmon is a salt water fish, but propagates in fresh water, in lakes, and heads of streams and rivers. Salmon return yearly to the place where they were propogated, causing what are called salmon runs. There are many kinds of salmon, good, better, best. The best, "silver sides;" the largest, "Chenook." The best are used at home in local markets; the second grade is shipped east (cold storage and packed); the poorest—hump backed, dog faced and common—are canned for the world's markets.

Needed Help.—Passing Redlands we heard that at Old Nine Mile Ranch the grass on hill was good. Arriving, found sheep and a herder there. "Yes," said he, "up on the hill the grass is good." We took our stock up and hobbled them. The herder going early found his horse had got fouled with the lariat and was down. He cut it and the horse rolled down the hill and was unable to get up. He came into camp, told his trouble, asked us (Bacon and I) to go up and help him. Bacon said, "I'm going ahead. No time. Good by." Said I, "I'll go and see what we can do." We lifted the horse up, it lunged and fell down the mountain. Examination showed that its back was broken, so we ended its existence with a revolver. Said the herder, "I'm at a loss; can't go forward with the sheep; no way to take camp things.

I'll give you my revolver and $2.50 cash to haul my outfit to Red Bluff." I did so. We never heard of Bacon afterward.

CHAPTER XVI.

Down the Sacramento Valley.

Late Gov. Stanford's Big Farm.—When passing through the town of Red Bluff it was suggested that we visit late Gov. Stanford's noted farm and winery. Crossing the Sacramento to the east we first saw oranges growing out doors. A few miles drive, on good roads, brought us to the Vina R. R. station. We introduced ourselves to the manager (Mrs. Stanford lives at College Farm, a place near San Jose) he kindly showed us around. The horse farm, 150 fine bred young horses, barns, stables, race track, etc. Then down to the Holstein dairy of 100 cows. They have their own creamery, got samples of their cream, butter, milk; saw them separating cream 30 minutes after it was milked. Latest improved machinery for everything except milking; that was done in the good old way. Then through their grapery of 3,000 acres. Then through their winery, the largest private bonded warehouse in the U. S. They said they "used 300 horses on the ranch." "The ranch is 6 miles long and 2 miles wide." They raise also wheat, alfalfa, timothy and clover. They have 3,000 hogs to which they feed the offal of the winery and the skimmed milk. They raise hundreds of ducks, geese, chickens, turkeys, etc. All persons living in Vina are directly or indirectly connected with or about the Stanford Farm, one of the cream spots of our earth; surrounding it the country is barren and useless. This was on Thursday, November 22, 1894.

Experience 15.—Grape and Green Walnut Diet.

In the Sacramento Valley agents and peddlers are not admitted to the *large ranch houses*. The tenants have no cash and but little to eat. Revenue being cut off, our money soon gone, hunger came over us; the grapes were left ungathered—too cheap. We asked for a few but were refused. I simply stepped over the fence, with burlap sack in hand, and filled it with grapes. Ranchman raged and threatened to arrest me; I retorted that my family was hungry. We gathered walnuts from trees alongside the road, lived 6 days on grapes and green walnuts, and traveled 150 miles on them. Grapes and green walnuts are good; but having to exist on them, alone for days together a person's stomach sickens; so did ours.

Experience No. 16.—The Battle.

Sacramento is a valley of big ranches, houses far apart, small dead towns often, but N. G. for work. We approached a large castle (a house) in center of a ranch of 30,000 (thirty thousand) acres. I hunted up the foreman and asked for work. He refused to give me any. Told him of our embarrassment—*no money, no food, no horse feed*, in need of nutriment for my family! Said he "did not care; we do not feed wagon tramps, so move on!" I refused and said. "I'll take grain from your bins, and hay from your rick, if you won't give me work to pay for it! Feed I'll have! Team can't travel without it." He, seeing my determination, said, "Carry out a little hay to your crow-baits!" I said, "I must have some barley also!" "Well, take your own sack, go out to the stable and tell the boss there to let you have a feed of grain." I did so. The grain boss said, "How much?" I said, "Put it in; I'll tell you when to stop." When the sack was full I said, "Stop, quick!" Then I went to the foreman again, and asked for food for my family. He said, "No; I've given you enough!" I said, "We will have a good breakfast tomorrow morning, and don't you fear!" Before daylight I was up and dressed, going to get a breakfast for my starving family. I could see chickens roosting up in a tree, so I up with a club and let drive at them. Presently I heard the clicking of a gun being cocked, and a voice in thunder tones call out, "You go nearer those chickens, I'll fill you with shot!" I turned and started for the speaker, club in hand. He disappeared around the grain elevator. To head him off I went around the opposite way, in time to see him again disappearing around his big house. Climbing the opposite fence a race for the rear commenced. I had become interested in the **flying Dutchman**. I met him; he dodged into the blacksmith shop, I after him. We came together; he dropped his shot gun and begged, saying "he did not intend to shoot me." In earnest tones I portrayed the situation—my starving family, I not being able to get work. Said he, "I now understand your dilemma, and can't blame you." Said I, "This is Thursday, Nov. 29—Thanksgiving, and we have nothing to be thankful for, except *health*." Said he, "You come into the house; I will give you some food." "No," said I, "but I will send in my little girl; don't you detain her a minute." (Had I gone into his house he might have turned a key and telephoned for an officer, and having money I would not now be in New York.) Our girl soon returned with an armful; again returned by invitation and made four trips. Result—roast turkey, roast beef, roast pork, stuffed lamb, chicken pot pie, baked potatoes, mashed potatoes, bread, butter, fruit, corn bread, plum pudding, pie, cake, cheese, potatoes, flour, beets, sugar, beans, syrup, onions, carrots, etc. We say, reader, we were loaded for a seige. We were thankful, and soon after our feast started forward, canvassing the towns for work, but found none.

The Roads.—The bottoms are low and level; the rivers all diked to hold back the water. At Mariesville the city is 10 feet below the bottom of the river; high dikes protect the city. The highways are on the dikes to make travel possible. These bottoms are overflowed yearly.

Sacramento, Cal.—**Dec. 3d.**—Not caring to have Salem experience repeated we only went round the fine capitol building, with its beautiful grounds, the finest we ever saw. In crossing America we have passed through 9 capitols—Salem, Sacramento, Carson City, Salt Lake City, Denver, Springfield, Indianapolis, Columbus and Albany.

Arriving at Stockton we were welcomed by a

terrific wind and heavy rain storm, flooding the streets and making the roads muddy, in the clay bottoms almost impassable. Passing Mountain House the hills were slippery and bad. At Livermore the roads were better; 'tis a nice valley there. At Haywards we got our first view of salt water. We arrived in Oakland, Dec. 17. Crossed the Creek Route Ferry. Cost us 85c. to cross the Bay, leaving us with 85c. cash.

Reporters got interviews and sketches, and advised us to go to the livery stable corner of New Montgomery and Mission Streets and await results. This we did.

In a House on Wheels.—A JOURNEY OF 1,200 MILES MADE BY M. LASLEY, AN UPHOLSTERER, AND HIS FAMILY.—Calm courage of a true wife who would rather share her husband's fortunes than to stay at home and wait. When Lasley's house appeared on our streets business of all kinds stopped. Every person was awe stricken? What is it? When first seen they had Market Street blocked solid. The children say "they enjoyed the trip." Their house is wonderfully arranged for comfort; fitted like a traveling palace car. They expect to continue their trip south, soon as the weather clears. The house is 12 feet long, 6 high, and 5 wide, with doors and windows. Camp stove, folding table and bed, lockers, commmode, chairs, etc. They have endured extreme hardships on their trip.—*San Francisco Examiner*, Dec. 18, 1894.

CHAPTER XVII.

Winter in San Francisco.—Rain! Rain! It commenced about Dec. 10th, and the time was well used. Our clothing became wet, our bedding damp. I had looked for work, but none found. Cheerless the outlook when I wrote,

Sonnet to My Last Penny.

The fates decree that I must say farewell
To thee, my cherished one, whom I would fain
Within the precincts of my purse retain
A little longer. Fancy dare not dwell
Upon the blank which thy departure makes
In my poor pocket, which, when thou hast left,
Of money will be utterly bereft.
Ah! even hope my fainting heart forsakes,
And vanishes with thee; for where to turn
To find another such I've yet to learn!
Yet, after all, it really is a wonder
That thou hast been so long my constant mate
When all my friends have fled. Oh, cruel fate,
That drives us two so far asunder!

Experience No. 17.—Hopes Deferred.

I went to the mayor (Sutro), told his clerk of my starving family. "I've no work, can't get any." Said he, "I am sorry; thousands just in same condition; good day. No cash to spare." I went to the relief societies, their reply "God bless you brother, our ability is limited, our treasury empty, go in peace; may heaven bless you." Applied to Salvation Army relief headquarters. Said, "Can't help any more poor; you're no better than others; thousands worse off than you; God bless you; Good by." Then applied to Salvation Army Capt. Wm. Day, Assistant Editor *War Cry*, a person I knew when I had money and he doing carpenter work in Port Angeles, Wash., before he married a Salvation Army Captain and was promoted from private in rear rank to be Assistant Editor of *The War Cry*. He received me kindly; but when I told of our sufferings, and asked him to assist me a little, he said, " I am busted; not got a cent!" I applied to Street Cleaning Department for employment as sweeper. In replying to questions which all applicants must answer all went well till "How long have you been in 'Frisco?" was asked. I replied, "Four days." The clerk's jaw dropped; he tore up the application, saying, "We never give work to new comers, but I'll tell you; you go down and see the Merchants' S. C. D. Here is their address. It's a long way, take street car, 'tis raining. Good by." No money, so I walked. Saw ths clerk; same reply: "Not here long enough. Say, just you call on Mrs. ——, President of the

Ladies' Christian Aid Society; they can put you on." I called; beautiful talking lady; asked me all the questions she could think of about my trip and family and said "Quite interesting!" When I told her of my starving family she changed tune and said, "Too bad! I'm sorry. Good by. 'Tis my busy day!" I returned to the M. S. C. Dept., reported how I was received. Said the clerk: "I will help you; take this." He wrote: "Order No. — Put bearer on half time, three days a week, for two weeks." To S. C. Dept.; they booked me. Said I, "When can I commence?" "Well, there are 600 ahead of you, and we put on about 100 a month; you can call again about next June." I became wiser, but weaker (nothing to eat for two days), I returned to stable.

A Change Took Place.—"Mary," said I, "we are going to change (to jail, may be). I am going to open these doors, push our house out upon the street, build a fire in our stove, dry our house ('tis musty), and cook a little grub. You have some raw material." "Yes, potatoes, coffee, onions." Out it went; the fire soon dried and warmed us. (Frisco has no wood or coal heating stoves.) A crowd soon gathered about us; the questions put to us were many; they heard of our starving condition. I stood near the front of our house, curious persons interviewed my family. ' The crowd was immense. Making my way through to the door, a gleam of hope was upon my sweet wife's face. Said she: "Look here!" The table was loaded with provisions, and more were upon the floor. Not being able to contain myself I dropped upon my knees and thanked God for our deliverance from starvation. I suggested that we return into the stable. The stable door closing upon the crowd, we invoiced our provisions—10 pounds cooked beef, potatoes, cooked ham, turkey, pies, cakes, cookies, bread, butter, coffee, sugar, plum pudding, pyramid cake, a layer cake, etc. Where it all came from we never found out, but we ate it with thankful hearts. Money also was given to the children, amounting to $8.30.

Our First Sketch Book.—"Mary, let's get a book printed to answer these questions and not be talked to death." She consented, providing I sold them. As soon as the printers found I had no money they said, "No." Hunted for three days receiving many rebuffs, but upon going into a small job office, proprietor said, "It isn't business, but I'll print you 1,000 copies; you pay as you sell them." I left my copy and returned happy. A gentleman suggested that I drive up to Kearney St. I did so, and stopped at a clothing house for an ad. (We had put upon our house, "Busted! No grub! No work!")

Returning, I Saw a Jam.—Street cars blocked, express wagons, trucks, carriages and cabs had stopped, people had climbed up to be able to see our house and family! I worked through the the crowd, and found people upon the wheels, between the horse, on the tongue, and behind them. I took the lines, shouted, "Look out!" we moved. Arriving at the stable, wife said, "See what was thrown in here while you were in that store!" Counting we found $38.90! Rich—suddenly from starvation to plenty! Yes, we were indeed very thankful.

Street Work.—Into the street we went again. I had had photos of our outfit taken, and now being ready, we **opened fire upon the crowd.** Our books, 15c. each; photos, 25c. We sold $15.00 worth the first evening. January 5, 1895.

Winter Quarters.—Found P. O. lot corner of Seventh and Mission Streets; got permission to put my outfit in it; worked the streets (free street license); did well.

New Start Southward.—Rain subsiding again we started south. Jan. 28th at San Jose; Feb.

we arrived at Oakland, worked the streets.

Wife and I decided I had better go by steamship (on cut rates, $2.50 steerage) up to Seattle to see about our claim. Did so, and was gone four weeks before I got back on same rates. Found the attorney had lied, trip n. g. My brave wife and children worked the streets selling our book and photos to live, protected at night by our dog Nig. I returned March 28 poorer in pocket but richer in experience. Encountered two storms at sea. April 1st we recrossed bay to enclosed sand lot. Not on street with outfit after April 12th. Our Viola sold the books outside—amount received 50c. to $2.00. She visited *alone* Golden Gate Park, Cliff House and Sutro Heights. I got a few jobs at upholstering. [During our seclusion I helped to organize and became secretary of the World's Christian Co-operative Society.]

Experience No. 18.—A Crowning Event.

We procured a fine doctor and a good nurse, also clothing and other accessories. A child was born to us in our *only house on wheels*—a healthy, bright-eyed girl baby. The papers got wind of the event, and Lo! presents, delicacies, and money poured in upon us. The child has grown till now, Feb. 9, 1898, she is a beautiful, rosy cheeked, healthy child, has but few equals. We named her for her birthplace, Francisco.

New Departure.—"Now, husband, in 2 weeks I desire to start forward." [Business men advised us to take our house on wheels, go and see the eastern country, travel and enjoy yourselves; you will make good money selling your books; by and by come back to 'Frisco and enjoy life.]

CHAPTER XVIII.
Our Western Coast States.

All the best land has long since been gobbled by railroads and speculators, and none but the poorest left. Only a very small portion of the coast States lands are tillable. The lands of California, Oregon and Washington generally are motgaged. The only valley in Oregon of much value is the Willamette, formerly an inland sea, and is generally very level; soil, good or poor—black soil, sand or gravel; crops variable according to soil; farmers mostly poor and stingy. *No cash*. Rogue River Valley is mostly fruit raising; the railroads take all profits. On the coast north of 'Frisco it is wet and foggy in the fall, winter and spring—rubber clothing used. In the summer it is very dry. **NO PLACE IN CALIFORNIA FOR A POOR MAN.** For hunting, no country like the Western coast. Fishing for sport *is fine*; profits, *none*. If you have a good job, *hold it*; no opening, sure, out West.

Reliable information about mining in the West, Alaska and other places free for 4 cents in stamps; address us.

" **To Cross America.**—Arrangements have been made, and the Lasley's, with their Traveling Palace, will try the perilous trip of taking it aross the continent to New York City."—Condensed clipping from *The San Francisco Examiner*, June 5, 1895.

CHAPTER XIX.
Eastward Ho!

June 6th, 1895.—Our larder was full, we had 400 books, $1.25 in cash and lots of grit. We started eastward *via* Haywards and Stockton. The roads were almost impassable owing to high water. In some places the bed of the road was covered with water; we were guiding our team by the willows that were on either side, keeping as near the middle as possible.

Broken Dikes.—For miles the valleys were covered deep with water, the overflow of the San Juan and Sacramento Rivers. The road we traveled was in the midst of an inland sea. Were glad when we reached high ground on the east side of the Sacramento Valley. Grass for our team was much better than when we went through in December. We passed through Stanford's land grant of 100 square miles.

Change in Camp.—"I say, Mr. House on Wheels, we'll camp with you tonight!" So saying, three roughly dressed men alighted from as many wagons while the fourth one of the party was a woman about 35 years old and *non compus mentus*. We laid the fence down and staked our horses in the pasture, little caring who owned it or where they lived. We had retired and were just dropping to sleep when a voice said, "Get up; take your horses and get out of here quick, or I'll blow your head off!" We heard the clicking of guns; I drew my revolvers, got up, opened the door slightly and looked out.

I saw two men in white about twenty feet away. I heard "Get your team, and git, or we'll fire on you;" "Don't shoot, don't; I'll leave." Presently a third man appeared, rifle in hand. He threw the harness on his horses (which he had left tied to his wagon, showing a plot. I had said to my wife, "We will watch that fellow; why did he not put his horses out on grass, as we did?") and back on the road he drove fast; bang, bang, bang, his horses' feet sounded on the still air. On inquiry we found that the son and brother had foiled the plan of this brute. Next morning they (father, son and daughter) asked permission to travel with us. We told them "the road was free." They kept with us till we got to Carson sinks; they got ranch work and stopped; we went on slowly.

THE SIERRA NEVADA MTS.

From Placerville to the American River, then up the rough, snow-capped mountain, being the first team over this season; cutting the snow and ice to be able to cross at all, we were told "we could not get over too early;" but we tried, and won at Summit, 8,000 feet, June 19, 1895. Down, down, quick down, till shortly we arrived down in Strawberry valley, crossed the line of California into Nevada, around noted Lake Tahoe, a magnificent body of water. The walls perpendicular in places. In one place the road is hung over the face of the ledge. Signs read "Don't ride over trestle, danger, etc." All of us rode; we were used to danger.

While on the top of the range the children picked flowers with one hand and put the other one in the snow banks.

From the lake we traveled uphill three miles. While coming up Mary cooked supper—fried meat, made biscuits, coffee and fried potatoes, etc., when camped at Hilltop, 900 feet above Tahoe, supper was ready to eat.

If space would allow would like to describe the flume,

eleven miles long, from hilltop down to Carson City, which carries down lumber, cordwood, railroad ties and poles, hauled from the mill on the lake or from adjacent hills. Some places the flume is nearly level, other places about 30 degrees pitch; at places the road goes under the flume, at other places over it, always near.

Arriving at Nevada's Capital City, Friday, June 21, 1895, we camped upon the public square, opposite the State Capitol—distance from 'Frisco by road, 248 miles.

A NIGHT ATTACK.—EX. NO. 19.

No, reader, not Indians this time; although at times along our road we slept upon our arms. Not wolves, either, although they often made it sound doleful with their howling; but mosquitoes. We had camped upon a beautiful grassy spot near the Carson river; the day had been rather warm; no flies, no bugs. So at this spot some eight or ten teams had camped for the night upon the grass. At early supper time the ranchmen came in from haying, wearing netting over their faces outside their broad-brim hats. Said one: "Boys, you are welcome to stay, but mosquitoes will eat you up." About half an hour before sundown the horses quit eating grass, commenced stamping, then rolling and rubbing. Going to the ranchman, we found he charged $1.00 to put teams in his stable over night. Several, glad to protect their teams, paid this $1.00. Removing the horses soon brought the mosquitoes into camp. (Some were cooking supper, others eating, some making their beds, some washing dishes, etc.) Oh, the change! The air was black with them; everybody stopped to fight them. Smudges did no good, tents no protection; horses came running into camp for protection; dogs howled, cows lowed and oxen dug up the ground. Women and children cried from the bites; men cursed and swore; some started for the hills (a mile away) and camped out there over night; others smothered themselves in bedclothes, etc. Cousins took shelter and worked to pay for it. We hitched up, pulled out into the hills, placed eight miles behind us, then stopped. We had escaped. Next day one of the campers overtook us. He said he was the last to leave. They stood it till after midnight, and so he pulled out; that all but us had taken the wrong road, and their party became divided, never to meet again.

WHITE PLAINS.

Dear reader, you must know something of geography to appreciate the country about to be described. We are now in the lowest place in the State of Nevada, the ground raising in all directions into mountains, the land for miles around dead level. The Carson River flowing from the Sierra Nevadas east and sinking in the sands forms the sink of the Carson (in the southern part of the basin). The Humboldt River forms the Humboldt Lake (in fact, a series of small pools). This river rises in the Humboldt mountain, flows southwest; very, very crooked; its valley from 200 feet to ten miles wide; sandy. Occasionally you encounter knolls of loose, dry sands, always shifting, making traveling hard—direction hard to follow. Suddenly, too, the ground changes; you cross an old lava bed, sand ceases, ground flat and smooth; hard as a stone; white crust, fine going, after the hot, dry, loose sand (a compound of salt and alkali). The light hurts our eyes. We exclaim "white plains."

WATER FAMINE.—EX. NO. 20.

We have gone hungry, been cold, wet and worn out, but none of these compare with going thirsty. 'Tis now the 29th of June. The thermometer 110 degrees in the shade. No habitation; no trees; no springs. (The Central Pacific Railroad alongside wagon road.) Not having learned at Wadsworth the condition of the barren country, we were unprepared for THE WATER FAMINE. We had brought only a gallon of water. Day hot, travel slow, sand heavy, we walked a good part of the forenoon and our water was soon gone. Saw section men on the road; went and asked the foresaid: "No, we don't give water away" (the section man, an American, for a little water for my family. He men were Chinamen). I asked if I could get some water at the section house when we came to it. He said "No." We drove on. Soon a curve in the road showed us the section house, five miles away. Hopes brightened, only to be dulled by slow travel hour after an hour passed. Children cried for water; our lips were parched, our tongues swollen, suffering agony. Finally at 3 p. m. we reached the section house. Everything locked and chained up; the water tank down in the ground covered heavily and door chained shut. Procuring a crowbar, I soon had the door off its hinges. Cautiously we sipped the water by spoonfuls until all of us were revived. Then our horses and faithful dog had the same treatment. Reader, did you say "were we not afraid of the boss coming?" Well, no; necessity knows no law—"self-preservation first law of nature" under conditions like these. Even cowards would fight. We fed the team, cooked dinner and started forward; slow travel; darkness came on, wolves howled about us; then again our water gave out and the pangs of thirst came on, but not so bad; it was a little cooler. At 10 o'clock a building hove in sight. Approaching it, we found it to be an abandoned salt works. We found barrels with fluid in them. Knowing animal sagacity, we tried it.

TESTING WATER BY USE OF DOG AND HORSES.

I took my dog in my arms, went to a barrel containing fluid, showed it to him; he scrambled, fearing I was going to put him in it. To next and next-same way. Finally he did not care. As we approached one (my heart beat high) he put his paws upon the rim and commenced to drink. This one was the only one he would touch. I then took one of our horses and led it alongside of the barrels. He refused till he came to the same one chosen by our dog. With a bucket soon watered our team and our dog. Our own thirst was also quenched. (We took no supper, but, tired, we went to bed.) My home made register told us only fifteen miles to-day; 3.30 a. m., at break of day, was up; examination showed this barrel contained water condensed from steam and very stagnant.

A TURNCOAT (FRIEND).—EX. NO. 21.

After seeing the water we could not drink it; so pushed forward seven miles to Hot Springs; water fine to drink after it cools; but so hot in the spring that flesh will cook in it. Next to a station house, five miles. They refused us water, so I took it by force. Water, feed and dinner, then forward, going down a steep pitch bluff for fifty feet, a hard level bottom was struck. A station soon in sight. We stopped. Going into the place I found the telegraph operator. Said I: "Sir, can I get some water, please, for our team and family over night?" "No," said he, "we don't water wagon tramps; 'tis only a mile over to the lake; the water is not very rank; you can go over there. Good night." An Irish section boss came in as I was going out. I asked him also for water. "Well, we are rather short, but we might spare a little for your family to drink." "I say no; go over to the lake; our water is low; good day," cried the operator. Passing the back door of the section house, ho the commotion. Two little girls saw our HOUSE ON WHEELS and called out: "Oh, papa, here is the HOUSE ON WHEELS we have been expecting." Presto, change. "I say, mister. Stop; drive your horses alongside the shed for protection from the wind; put your horses in the stable; get water out of the tank (when it is gone we can get lots more). Here is all the wood you want." His family coming out to see us, insisted upon us staying over night and over next day (Sunday) and taking dinner with them, which we did. All four of them were musicians and entertained us well. We spent a Sunday long to be remembered. Name, Mr. Wm. Wrich, White Plains, Nevada. Our route now was up Humboldt River Valley. Varied was our experience, fording the river in dangerous places, three times experiencing encounters with horse thieves, being surrounded by coyotes, being lost in the sand hills over night, being lost on the river among the marshes and swamped in the mud flats; attacked again by mosquitoes and marsh flies; also attacked in the hills by sand flies. Oh, horrors! Few ranches and fewer towns; little water and hard to get.

RABBIT HUNT AT SLOAN'S RANCH, NEAR WINNEMUCCA, NEV., JULY 8, 1895.

('Tis a Paradise for Rabbits.)

Desiring some fine sport, I took the gun and started down the grade toward the river. The ranchman, seeing me, came running out of the house. "Stop!" cried he; "no use of a gun in here." "Only going to kill a few rabbits," said I. "Hold!" said he; "no use wasting powder. I'll show you how I kill rabbits." At that we had approached the bottom, rabbits sporting everywhere. The sight was too tempting. I let drive with one load and killed two young rabbits. He protested. "Don't waste powder. Call your dog. Go over the bridge. I'll stay on the bridge and kill them." My dog Nig and I crossed the bridge on to an island. Oh, the rabbits! The dog in his glory, started a drove of rabbits for the bridge, where the ranchman was in hiding behind a gate. They had to pass; he laid upon them, striking right and left. The dog, seeing the man clubbing, stopped to look. I called the dog back and soon had another drove crossing the bridge. Again he plied his club. We repeated this several times, with the result that I gathered up eighteen. They were all young, half-grown jack rabbits, fine eating,

PRICE OF HORSES IN NEVADA.

Approaching Lockwood, parties desired to sell us

horses. Inquiry developed that horses were very cheap. Indians offered to go on to the range and bring us horses for $2 per head. Becoming interested I hunted up some of the horse raisers to get a few facts, and found that the demand for horses had ceased, and the ranges in Nevada, Oregon and Idaho had become overstocked, and that there was a united effort of the raisers to reduce the number to save the range. So lots of hogs were bought, turned loose upon the range and hunters were hired to kill range horses to be devoured by the hogs for food Range horses only $1.50 to $5 each, and no demand at that The first horse buyers we saw was in central Illinois. From the Mississippi River west horse flesh is cheap, and further west the lower it is.

After untold hardships we arrived at Battle Mountain station, July 12; sold $2.25 books and pictures: canvassed town for work; found some upholstering at hotel, Mrs. Huntsman, prop.

TEAM STRAYED, LOST OR STOLEN.

I worked over a mattress in the afternoon. Team stayed around well. At midnight looked for them, and they were gone. At daylight I hired a pony and rode back twelve miles, then among the hills, and at dark found them cached away. I took them home and watched them close. Riding in the hot sun overcame me and for two days I tossed with fever, then rallied and commenced to work again. Earned $3.50 cash and a supper for all of us. Reaction set in.

DOWN WITH MOUNTAIN FEVER.

For the next four weeks I suffered with mountain fever, not being able to sit up. My wife suggested I lie down and she would drive the team, and so up and down the mountains and over the plains she drove. What happened I know but little and cared less. Five weeks passed before I regained health. The journal shows she drove 211 miles with me sick in bed. In bad places Viola assisted in getting the team along. Viola and wife cared for team also. Finally the promontory appears. The salt air of Salt Lake was fine.

BUENA VISTA.

Of all the charming things that impressed our minds was the beautiful Salt Lake Valley, Utah. As first viewed from the barren hills above Corrin it is beyond description, coming from those desolate, barren plains of Nevada into that magnificent garden spot, the oasis in the American desert. The Mormon-made paradise, Salt Lake Valley, is a sight long to be remembered. We feasted upon their fruits, melons, corn, garden truck, honey, creamery butter, cheese, milk, eggs and poultry. After entering the valley at Brigham we feasted in it, rested and enjoyed ourselves with the people until the 23d of August, 1895,

VARIED EXPERIENCES.

At Salt Lake City we visited the Tabernacle, Temple, Beehive, Eagle Gate, Sealing House, old city wall, hot springs, &c. At Springville we attended a campfire of Indian War veterans. Leaving the Jordan valley, we headed for Grand Junction, Colo., across 125 miles of desert, having more hardships of hunger and thirst, crossing the dangerous Green River ford, letting our house down steep sand washes by aid of ropes, and going down steep, dangerous canyons over rocks and down deep gorges for water. On September 18 we arrived at Grand Junction, another oasis in the desert. We rested a couple of days up Grand River. Crossing a high mountain on September 21 we were caught in a snowstorm. Oh, how it snowed! Being on the very top the next day we easily came down out of it. Down on the river it had rained. At Glenwood Springs, September 27, a summer resort; up Roaring Fork, then across to Eagle River, over Sheephorn Range, on to the Blue Cross Divide to Grand River, up to Hot Springs, near the foot of Continental Divide, September 28, 1895.

HARD CLIMB.

Up the mountain side high, higher, higher; no level place, road fairly good, some spots of snow, all day up, up. At dark we camped, put our horses into an old cabin, in which we found hay and used for feed. We were then at the perpetual snow line, and it was very cold. Early next morning was up and ready for more climbing over the ice until finally by using ropes we gained the summit of the range, two and a quarter miles above sea level. Cold, and the wind, how it howled on the summit! Then immediately down on the east side it descends very quickly 3,000 feet down, down, down, it being harder on us to go down than up and more dangerous. Down—up, up—down, across until the wide plains east of the mountains are in view. We felt relieved when our eyes beheld Denver City, our Mecca, and we drove into it on Saturday evening, October 12, 1895.

Total distance traveled, 2,775 miles. We had crossed eighteen mountain ranges and thirteen divides.

OUR FINANCES OF 1895.

Four hundred of our books, $1.25 and $8.50, at Battle Mountain, aided us to reach Salt Lake City; books and pictures gone, 90c. yet in cash. Bought material and made Indian eye salve; also material for marking silver and steel and a camp solder. These we traded for provisions or sold for cash. Arriving at Denver, Colo., we had 75c. in cash.

A HARD STRUGGLE.

Our team dies. Our horses had got alkalied, and on the second day after reaching Denver one of them died. We were thankful it was not one of our children, and a few weeks after this the other horse died. So we lecided to winter near Denver, and we thought it best to vacate our house on wheels and try gold prospecting in the new gold camp in the foothills west of Denver. A friend gave me a broncho, and in breaking him he threw me and broke my collar bone. Not daunted, with shoulder bound up, I went up into the new camp, and with pick I prospected; but upon the icy mountain I slipped, fell and broke a rib; but still I stayed. Joy! Two weeks after this who should I see getting off the train near our camp but my wife and children. My wife said: "I just could not stand it any longer, so borrowed the cash and here we are." She had written she was coming, and I had prepared in part a cabin, but did not expect them so soon. I was delighted to see them. Soon, with the aid of my family, I, with one arm, had a fine, comfortable stone cabin for us, dug out of the mountain, covered with lumber, then cloth and dirt, size 25x14 feet. My wife began baking on her stove, and soon was supplying the miners with bread, pies, cakes, crullers, &c. Viola carried them to their cabins. I took a job digging a prospect hole for $25. I hired a man to do the job, and cleared $14. I sent to Denver and got a few things to sell to the miners, such as tobacco, flour, bacon, sugar, salt, matches, candles, &c., at good profit. Each day I closed out, and each day I procured a new supply. Soon I added fresh beef, butter, eggs, lard, cigars and meats, pickles, fruit, &c. I staked more claims, did surveying claims, formed mining companies, and was one of the mainstays in camp. Time passed and May came. I was aware the camp was no good for a poor man, as the pay ore was too deep. So we hunted up a speculator, sold my six holes in the ground for $50, closed out personal effects, went to Denver, bought a good 2,500-pound team and had $75 to get ready for the road again. My broken bones had united. We repaired our house, bought a camera, had 500 books printed, put in $20 worth of notions to sell upon the road, and on May 28, 1896, started again for New York, via Texas.

HOPES BRIGHTEN.

Roads good, team fresh, spirits high, weather delightful. We visited the Garden of the Gods, near Colorado Springs; also visited Manitou Springs, the famous watering-place at the foot of Pike's Peak. Arrived at Pueblo June 8. Papered and refitted our house on wheels.

At Trinidad, Colo., on June 15. Over divide, down Cimerona Creek, at White's ranch, I traded a mule I had bought in Denver for a wild young horse, which I soon broke to work. Most of the settlements we passed through were Mexican. I learned my wife and daughter, Viola, to speak their language, and they took pleasure in selling our notions to them at good prices. Towns few and far apart, country being settled sparingly. Country stores 40 to 60 miles apart.

BIG RANCHES.

On June 26 we came to Texline, a small town and railroad station in northwest corner Panhandle, Texas. It was located on XIT ranch, called the State Capital Syndicate ranch. Capitalist built the Texas State Capitol Building for State lands located on northwest side of State. Size of ranch, 40 miles wide by 200 miles long, divided into seven divisions. It has thirty-nine windmills, employs a fence rider, two oilers and cowboys to each division. Each fence rider sees to and repairs 135 miles of wire fence. The fence cost $106 per mile. The divisions are all well stocked with different kinds of horned cattle. The old road runs diagonal through this ranch. There are also three towns located within its bounds, and several small ranches inclosed by their own fences (ranches of a few miles square they fenced in and went on). Very few springs on the northern part, and most of the water is brought to the surface by windmills.

DANGEROUS CROSSINGS.

We arrived at Tascosa, Tex., on Canadian River, Saturday, July 4. Canvassed town, sold notions. We were advised to cross the river (rainy season had commenced). We did so in evening; sure next morning crossing cut off, river up, no crossing again for six weeks; we safely on south side, so forward we went.

At Goodnights we saw the largest herd of Buffalo in United States. At Memphis, Tex., July 15. Creeks and Red River not fordable (rivers not very deep, but dangerous quick sands), so waited. Got few jobs to do. Put our horses on grass. On 21st arrived at Newlin, half a mile from Foard, on Red River. No crossing. On 23d river lowered. Nine teams waiting, five on one side, four on other.

QUICKSANDS.

"I am going across," said I. "If you do, so do we," said they. All the men stripped off outer clothing, waded in, and tried the crossing. We sank to our knees, then to our hips, then to our waists in the sand. We finally settled the sand, and the bottom became firm. We crossed with horses first to try the bottom. Some of them reared and plunged; others laid down. Our large, tall horses did nicely. I helped draw five outfits across. Then came our house on wheels. The water was breast deep to me. My team snorted and pawed. I grabbed the harness, and away we went. Our house floated—not six inches of water on floor. We crossed the best of all, with many cheers. All being across safe, we were thankful. My wife and children said they enjoyed the excitement, but excuse me. We arrived at Sherman (Cyclone) City Aug. 15.

(Headlines of papers)
"HOUSE ON WHEELS in Town from Washing-

ton. Three Summers en Route. Distance Traveled, 3,700 miles." "Sherman Post," Aug. 16, 1896.

"HOUSE ON WHEELS. A Peculiar Journey Across the Continent."
"Sherman (Tex.) Democrat," Aug. 15, 1896.

We enjoyed two three-day picnics at Sherman. Heat, 117 degrees in the shade. At Greenville, Aug. 26.

CHANGED EXPERIENCE. EX. NO. 24.

It causes us to smile to see the pomposity of some city officials. At Greenville, wishing to rest our team for a few days, I decided to effect a change in the experience, as variety is the spice of our lives. We camped on the public square four days, and during the time I took in dimes as a mind reader. We were leaving the square when the collector demanded an occupation tax, stating I was fortune telling. I denied it, and refused to be taxed as such. He reported me to his brother officers, and a warrant was issued for my arrest. I gave bond, and was on hand for trial. After lots of bullragging the prosecuting attorneys rested; so did I. The Mayor declared the city failed to make a case, and I was at liberty. All the parties I gave a reading to were well satisfied and pleased.

On Sunday we drove out to a grove to attend a camp meeting. A committee from the camp waited upon us to investigate report of mind reading. I read for them; they failed in their mission, and returned.

AN INJUNCTION.

Be not too quick to judge, my brother,
    For a kindred power you may feel;

Heavy burdens may be lifted,
  Two minds working at your wheel.
Let him know that you take an interest;
  It will not take him long to see
Whether you are a true well wisher
  Or a shamming Pharisee.

Do not turn your back upon him,
  Do not coldly walk away,
Just because you think you're made of
  Some superior kind of clay.

When you come to think about it,
  As sometimes we mortals must,
There is nothing very striking
  In the finest kind of dust.

NORTHWARD.

"Something unique in Paris."
"HOUSE ON WHEELS—A Family of Six."
"Travels 3,832 miles."
  "Paris Tribune," Sept. 2, 1896.

We had 1,000 of our books printed. We visited cotton compress bailers, cotton oil mills and factories, saw where they burned the negro. Sept. 14, started for St. Louis, via Indian Territory.

TEXAS PEOPLE.

They are the most religious people we ever met with. We did not hear a dozen oaths in the State. The masses are very poor, especially in the farming districts. The colored people own a large proportion of the farm lands. Many of the colored people have white tenants on their lands. Large syndicates own the grazing lands.

EYE CLOSER—VIOLA'S EXPERIENCE.

"Be careful, don't touch any of those green vines; they are poisonous," said I to the children. On Sept. 18, at Caddo, I. T., Viola complained of stinging. I knew it was poison. We gave antidotes and used lotions; could relieve, but not cure. Called in doctors, but they failed. At Coalgate, Sept. 21, Dr. Haskins volunteered to cure our child free, also free feed for our team. He used the strongest medicines known. The case stubbornly held out; her face was swollen, eyes closed and inflamed. Finally the color changed, case gave way, and gradually improved, leaving her eyes weak for a time. They were more careful

BABY FRANCES RUN OVER. EX. NO. 25.

We camped on the main street in Coalgate, I. T. Children played all round us. At dusk on Sept. 23 we heard the rattle of a team passing, clatter of hoofs, scream of a child. Jumping out we beheld our sixteen-month-old babe between the hind feet of a span of mules. The driver had not seen the child until he knocked her down with the wagon tongue, too late to save her. He stopped, I dove between his team, crowded the mules off the clothing of our child, handed the unhurt, but scared, babe to its mother, gave driver a talking to about carelessness. He offered to procure a doctor and pay bill. We examined babe, accepted his apology, and liberated him. Our child not even bruised.

CROSSING THE NATIONS, I. T.

Nothing special occurred (barring night attack of wolves and mosquitoes, camping out among bandits, crossing dangerous rivers, surrounded by deadly reptiles, breaking of the wagon tongue in dangerous place, the wheels breaking down, being misguided, etc.), until we arrived at Wagoner, I. T., Oct. 3.

SECOND TEAM DIES. EX. NO. 26.

a week past. Examination showed he was alkalied; might recover, but doubtful. Going out to hitch up the horses at Wagoner I found one dying and soon dead; other one sick. On the 7th he died. We were penniless, only little grub, no cash, no work to be gotten. Horses low priced, but no money to buy with. Upon our house we put notice: "Team wanted to draw our house on wheels to Venita."

NEW TEAMSTERS. EX. NO. 27.

One of our horses had not been feeling very well for Lots idle horses and men. They demanded pay in advance. I say, "I'll pay when job's done." On Oct 13th got man to haul our house to Venita, 40 miles, for $5. Arriving, I gave lecture on mind reading, and on our trip took up collection, sold few books, and paid our driver; dismissed him. Got another to haul us to Chetopa, Kas., 32 miles, for $1.75. Oct. 15, on street of Chetopa gave a silver lecture to large body of gold men; took up collection and sold books.

A NEW SET OF BONES CALLED A TEAM.

A gold man called next morn. Said he: "You are a silver advocate. I am for gold, but I am a man for all that. I heard your lecture; it suited me. I'll give you a pair of ponies." His son and I went out and got them. Oh, so poor, had to be helped up when laid down. We commenced to grain and care for them, and in a week were on the road again, from one town to next. At Joplin, Mo., we gave lectures on mind reading, politics, travel. Under pressure, my wife gave readings; did extra well. On Monday, Nov. 2, we arrived at Webb City, Mo. I gave silver lecture to big silver crowd, then sold the names of next President for 10c. each. On opening found McKinley's. They were disappointed. Stayed there till after election, then forward. Arrive at Springfield, Mo., Nov. 13,

OUR OLD HORSE BARNEY.

We were on the farmers' square lecturing, selling books, giving readings. I gave thirty-seven readings at 10c. Saturday afternoon I heard an auctioneer offering a horse for sale at a dollar. I offered $1.05, and got our old blind Barney. Now, 1899, he is 28 years old. At Springfield, Mo., we had traveled 4,337 miles. Now, March 1, 1899, our total is 8,065 miles. We have driven him 3,728 miles. A wonderful horse he is; used to be a race horse.

CHANGED MATES ON THE ROAD.

We traded our two ponies for one horse. Wore it out. Traded it for another, gave $2 to boot. He proved balky. You would laugh to see some resorts to make him pull; used him half a day, then traded. Then traded again. Then traded again—four times in twenty-four hours. Gave a revolver to boot. This one developed ringbone, so traded again. Then traded for a pair of mules, gave $2 to boot. Then the mules I traded for a nice fat mare, proved balky. I used her for 500 miles. At Little Washington, Pa., traded again, and gave a watch and 75c. cash to boot. This horse I now have. You can see old blind Barney has had twelve mates on this trip.

PROBLEM.

I am driving my eleventh horse on left side, my twentieth on the right. How many horses have I had on this trip? A prize for correct solution.

Springfield, Mo., is on the very top of the Ozark Mountains. The road follows the summit sawtooth fashion. Road in timber muddy; on prairie sandy and dry; on creek bottoms sticky loam. Hills very rocky and bad. Our travel was slow and hard. Towns few. At three school houses we gave entertainments; receipts $4 to $5 each. Passed through Union City, Mo., December 7. Roads improved. On December 9 we drove into St. Louis; stopped 1400 Broadway, corner Second Street. Camped over night. On the 10th down into the city. Got free permit to sell our books on the street. Sold $5 worth. Located on lot on Market Street, between 13th and 14th Streets.

HEADLINES OF PRESS.

"Over a Continent." "This Family Is Traveling in a House Wagon." "Their Appearance in St. Louis Attracted Much Attention."
    "St. Louis Star," Dec. 13, 1896.

"A Prairie Schooner." "A Regular '49er on the Streets of St. Louis." "With a family Making a Transcontinental Trip."
    "St. Louis Republican," Dec. 13, 1896.

"House on Wheels Looted by Thugs." "Latest Freaks of Crime." "Entire Family Lined Up and Robbed of $2.70 at Corner 17th and Chestnut Streets." "St. Louis Post-Dispatch," Dec. 12, 1896.

This last is a "Post-Dispatch" lie out of whole cloth. The reporter made fifty-seven statements and told fifty lies, making ONE BIG LIE.

Got 1,000 books printed. We sold books on the streets and did advertising for three firms, Harris, Dietz and Hilts, until January 5. We thought best to go up to Chicago, Ill.; crossed the Mississippi River on bridge. At Springfield, Ill., January 16, 1897, by special invitation, visited Lincoln's home on Sunday; his monument, State Capitol, &c., on Monday. Sold lots of books on street. We especially remember Mr. and Mrs. Johnson, Mrs. D. B. Ayers and Dr. Diller and father for kindnesses tendered us and favors shown.

A BLIZZARD.

On January 22 at Lincoln a northerner set in. It got cold, zero; 23d, 8 deg. below zero; 24th, 12 deg. below; 25th, 16 deg. below; 26th, 18 deg. below zero. Then it moderated. We traveled only in the middle of the day. February 1 at Pontiac. February 7 at Joliet. On Thursday, February 12, arrived at Chicago. Capt. White, of the London Museum, engaged us on sight for two weeks. Got 1,000 books and pictures printed. Distance from St. Louis by road, 340 miles.

On March 4 we started for Cincinnati, O. Through northern Indiana the mud was bad; took us three days to travel ten miles around Kankakee Swamp. Through Kokomo, Ind., March 24, 1897. March 27 at Indianapolis. Roads now pike. April 5 into Cincinnati. Distance from Chicago by road, 377 miles. Free street permit. Sold books. C. H. and D. R. R. gave us $1 an hour to carry an "ad." for them. We took a short trip over in Kentucky.

On April 16 forward for my old home in Cheshire, via Columbus. Roads built by the United States Government fine. On the 22d at Columbus; distance from Cincinnati, 133 miles. On May 8 arrived at my old home. Met relatives and friends. I had not been there in twenty-one years. We were well received. More invitations to dine than had time. On the 17th, by special request, I gave a lecture on our trip to a large audience in the Opera House. Said farewell to friends. On 18th at Athens; visited relatives; gave lecture in City Hall on 24th; attendance large. Now for Pittsburg, Pa. Road hilly. Sold our books every place. June 5 at Wheeling, W. Va. At Pittsburg June 14. Had 1,000 books printed. Total distance, 5,857 miles. From Cincinnati our route, 557 miles. Sold lots of books on the street; free permit.

ROBERT'S EXPERIMENT.

"Papa, let me hing (sing), please," said our little boy (after I had lectured one evening). I did so. "Now," said he, "I want penny." He collected 90c. He has sung in every city since then, with more or less success, till now he owns a United States Government $20 bond in his own name. He is proud of it, indeed. Says he's going to have another one. Every day he sings for a few pennies. He is a sure keeper; never spends his money; gets his spending money from papa or mamma.

We worked Pittsburg till June 25; then forward. On

June 30 at Erie, Pa.; distance, 150 miles. Streets free to us. Had 1,000 books and pictures printed. On July 7 at Buffalo, N. Y. Streets free. Saturday, July 10, city sweltered in heat; 98 deg. in shade. Sold books on streets till July 28; then drove up to Niagara Falls; enjoy open hospitality to everything. Sold lots of books and pictures. Had 2,000 books and pictures printed. On August 3 drove back to Buffalo; sold more books and did waiting. Became acquainted with Prof. Taylor and family, with whom we had many a pleasant evening.

A MEMORABLE DAY.

Tuesday, August 31, 1897, a babe was born to us, the second one in our HOUSE ON WHEELS.

HEADLINES OF NEWSPAPERS.

"Baby Born in the House on Wheels." "Addition to the Lasley Family." "Nice Nine-Pound Girl." "Will Have a Name Identifying Her with Buffalo." "Wagon Will Soon Move on Toward New York."

"Buffalo Courier Record," Sept. 5, 1897.

We had the best physician and nurse in the city. We named our babe Bonita Buffalo Lasley.

On September 9 my wife said: "Come, now for New York City." Roads good; team well rested. We attended Rochester, N. Y., fair on September 15. At Palmyra fair on September 21. (Fairs "N. G." for us.)

MY WIFE'S FIRST LECTURE.

At Syracuse Wednesday, September 29, 1897. We had got free street permit. I was selling books to a crowd around the front of our house by the team. Some well dressed women came to the door, looked in and made fun of the construction. It fired my wife. Going to the door she replied to the women. Then, having broken the ice and seeing about 500 people before her, she commenced to tell of our trip and to sell books. She did not stop for an hour and a half. I then insisted upon her stopping, and she consented reluctantly. The next day she could hardly make a sound, but she soon recovered. Since then she has addressed more than 100,000 people. She is a fine, enthusiastic speaker.

PRESS CLIPPINGS.

"A Palace on Wheels." "Curious Vehicle Visited Utica." "Long Trip Overland."
              "Utica Observer," Oct. 5, 1897.

"HOUSE ON WHEELS." "Family Traveling Across the Continent Stops at Little Falls."
              "The Evening Times," Oct. 7, 1897.

October 9 at Amsterdam. Had 2,000 books printed; also pictures. October 14 at Albany, N. Y.; on market square. Visited Troy City over Sunday, October 17. At Hudson on 20th. At Wappinger Falls on October

28. By invitation from Superintendent Goering we visited Sweet, Orr & Co.'s factory; fine one. On 30th at Newburgh. Had 1,000 books printed; also plates made of books. By invitation we visited the home factory of Sweet, Orr & Co.; very, very kind; only factories in the East that we have been invited to inspect. We carried an "ad." free as a compliment for them. November 5 at Tarrytown; they donated us flags to decorate our house with. Also bought lots of books. At Yonkers on November 6. We got 3,000 more books printed.

A CLOSE CALL BY FIRE.

On November 8 we had worked the streets at Yonkers and retired. At 2 A. M. we were routed by a rap. A voice said: "A big fire near you. Better get up. The stable is on fire!" Into part of my clothes I got, and asked assistance to move our house on to the street. That done, family safe; then for the horses and harness. The fire roared and blazed high. The fire department responded quickly, and the fire was confined to a saloon adjoining the stable. No damage to stable; only close call. We were frightened.

CHRISTENING.

Our Bonita Buffalo was baptized Sunday, November 14, 1897, in the First M. E. Church of Yonkers,

On November 15 wife and I visited New York City to get location, do some shopping and see the sights. Grand sights to us.

On November 17th we drove into New York City. Located at 150th street and Convent avenue. At city line, the police waved their hats and said, "Welcome, House on Wheels, into Greater New York."

A RED LETTER DAY

it was to us. We had accomplished something never before done—crossed America in a HOUSE ON WHEELS. Making our own way, having only $1.25 when leaving San Francisco. We felt relieved. We knew our history would be in demand. We felt, with proper attention, we could LIVE.

Thousands had told us we could not make the trip, and only six (up to St. Louis) had said of course we can; those six helped us more than a person can imagine. Thanks to them.

RECAPITULATION.

Distance, as we traveled, from Port Angeles, Wash., to San Francisco, 1,200 miles; days traveled, 65; daily average, $18\frac{1}{2}$ miles. Mountainous and rough country. San Francisco to Denver, Colo., 1,575 miles; days traveled 87; average, $18\frac{1}{3}$ miles; mountainous; deserts and sand. Denver to St. Louis, Mo. (via Texas), 1,810 miles; days traveled, 92½; average, 19½ miles; country generally level. St. Louis to New York, 2,081 miles; days traveled, 101; average, 20½ miles; roads generally good. Total distance, 6,666 miles; total days traveled, 346; average travel, about 19¼ miles.

In gathering items of interest for our complete book we left our line sometimes 100 miles to see and gather facts.

We have crossed 20 mountain ranges, 18 divides and 13 hills, some of them 8,500 feet high; forded 11 large rivers and ferried 12; have crossed 35 large bridges across rivers; have passed through three heavy wind storms, had the top blown off our house in less than a minute.

I have driven 285 miles with a broken tire, wired together. Have broken out four tongues and four double-trees, all the single trees; the neck-yoke is the one we started with.

OUR CYCLOMETER.

You would smile to hear many of the remarks we hear. Watch that crowd of nicely dressed men. They look around. Hear them. "Just see those fat, healthy children." "See that nice, blue-eyed woman." "Oh, say, Pete, just see that clock on the wheel, ha, ha, ha!" Reasonably, you expect well dressed, well groomed, well fed, polished-looking, smooth-shaven individuals to show that they were educated, instead of showing their ignorance by calling a mile register a clock, when reason would inform a thinking person that registers (not clocks) were attached to wheels; but as it is made out of a clock I excuse them. I used an old alarm clock; reconstructed it into a register. For a mile the hands register one hour. We note the time by the register when starting, again when stopped; difference in hours is the miles traveled. Each day I note in our journal the distance traveled, so 'tis no guesswork. Anything of importance is noted down—weather, cash receipts, kind of people and how we are treated by them; how officers act toward us; the business conditions of the people; accidents, etc. (This book is written with my journal before me.)

We did hope to print an illustrated book, but the cost is too great now for us; but it is our ambition. We have hundreds of pictures to select from.

NEWSPAPER HEADLINES CLIPPINGS.

"6,666 MILES IN A HOUSE ON WHEELS."
The Lasleys Came to This City From Port Angeles, Wash., in a Prairie Schooner. Crowds
See the Strange House.
—New York Herald, Nov. 22, 1897.

FAMILY FINDS FORTUNE IN ITS HOME ON WHEELS.

Evicted From His Farm on Puget Sound, Lasley Takes His Wife and Children all Over the Continent in a Van Drawn by Horses.

Now at 150th St. and Convent Ave.

New York Journal, Nov. 24, 1897.

LIFE IN A HOUSE ON WHEELS.

Home of the Lasleys Since 22d March, 1894.

New York World, Nov. 24, 1897.

Other New York papers had writeups, but the above suffice to show notice taken of our arrival in New York.

OUR NEW YORK EXPERIENCE.

We expected when arriving in New York to go into a museum for a few weeks, then sell our outfit as a curio to somebody and return West. So we called upon Huber. Said he: "I would like to engage you, but I see your children are all less than 15, so I can't; the law prohibits." We called upon Mr. Gerry. "No, not in any museum or playhouse here," said he. "You may rent a place, run it yourself, so you don't have music. Yes, you can sell your books upon the street, have your children along; no objection." We called upon the city officials. "No, you can't get upon our streets. No room. Cause too much attraction. No free permits to our streets. If you have the money to pay we will have a special act for you passed in the Council." "State your price," said I. "Call to-morrow. Good day." I called. The Councilman (of the ward I was in) was hunted up; application signed and paid for (more red tape); finally badge, tags and license given and $25.00 paid for it. Returned (to stable on 150th street). Ready; on to New York streets with our house, books and pictures; (Monopoly style), we raised the price to pay for the license. After selling enough half tone pictures to repay us for license and a few dollars extra we reduced the price of book and half tone to regular price—10c.

The police generally treated us nicely. Once in a while some new one (on the force) would try his powers. Once we were taken into Headquarters for investigation, only to be liberated, and the patrolman censured. While off the street we stayed from one to three weeks at a place, renting a stable for our horses and having a lot for our house. We worked the streets in our neighborhood, then changed to another location. We took part in the procession of Greater New York on January 1st, 1898. Our locations: 150th street and

Convent avenue; 132d street, near Third avenue; Forty-second street and Tenth avenue; Tenth avenue on Fourteenth street; Fifty-fifth street off Broadway; Peck's slip stables and No. 60 Cherry street, Carie's place.

WE BUILT ANOTHER HOUSE.

At Tenth avenue and Forty-second street one evening a rap we heard. Opening the door, a finely dressed man and woman were seen. "Good evening. We bought and read your book. I used to be out in Washington. We called to show our friendship; I find you speak the Chenook dialect," said the man. In conversation we learned he desired a job as a salesman; that his wife was in poor health, and to travel as we do would be desirable to both of them. We gave him a job helping us sell our books. After moving down to Tenth avenue off Fourteenth street we constructed another house upon the running gear of a wagon for this man and his wife (to travel with us, as we had decided by this time to see more of our world and to have company rather than to be alone). We agreed to own it together; he to buy the material, I to make it. Finally we got it inclosed, windows in, door hung and canvas-covered top. We changed to Fifty-fifth street off Broadway. We learned by this time that continuous company would not be agreeable to us; so decided to dissolve partnership. We offered to buy their half interest in the new house, but "they had become attached and their ambition was to travel;" so I offered to sell my half interest to them for $33.00 cash. They had no money. "Give us thirty days' time, please; here are our gold watches for security." So saying, he handed me a lady's gold watch, and taking his own off its chain, handed it to me. I examined them. Upon the face of his was his name—Edwin L. Bascom. A year and four months passed, and we hold the watches as mementoes. He may some day be able to redeem their watches. They had desired I make theirs a house on wheels. I said: "No. No opposition; we have the only house on wheels in the world, and it shall continue to be."

OUR COMPLETE BOOK.

On January 15th, 1898, the weather was so severe we decided not to work the streets till winter gave way, so rented stalls, got lot room at No. 60 Cherry street; decided to thoroughly overhaul our house and refit it for renewed travel, so rented rooms and commenced to enjoy a rest from visitors. We were not idle. I wrote a portion of our complete history of our trip. We had persons offer to criticise and correct our copy. I said: "No; this is not a literary work, but a plain statement of facts of our trip across America in our only house on wheels. We claim originality of expression, copying after no one."

After writing and correcting our own copy I went to the different publishing houses, and soon discovered New York publishers' prices high, so decided to do our own work. Publishers tried to dissuade me, saying "not being experienced, it would cost me more." I had been accustomed to opposition, so tried it; placed the copy in a printer's hands, read my proof; got an electrotyper to make the plates; bought my own paper from a paper house; got a press house to print them, a bindery to bind and trim them, and had 2,000 copies made as a trial. On counting the cost we had saved $115.00 on the lowest offer we had received from any of the publishers in the city.

Finding the cost to be so much, even doing as we did, we decided to publish our book in serial form; so eighty pages was the amount decided upon, and during 1898 thousands of copies sold.

OUR TRAVELS OF 1898.

Having rested ourselves and team for ten weeks; had had eighty pages of this book published. Our house refitted, March nearly gone, decided to go south and meet spring. On the 26th of March drove over to Newark, N. J.; bought a street permit, to learn after getting it we could sell upon the streets, but was not permitted to stop or attract a crowd; so the money was thrown away. We procured a lot in City center, and there in rear of the City Hall sold lots of our books. Imagine our surprise when selling our books to a crowd at 10c. to hear a voice say "I paid 15c. for my book and picture, and I would not take a dollar for them." That being the case, let me have one here, and here, and here one, and so on. After supplying the demands I turned to find who caused the commotion and saw Mr. Bascom. We learned they desired to travel in our company. We agreed; said we would leave on the 12th of April. Saying they would be on hand, he returned to New York. We waited till the 14th of April; then started at Elizabeth, free permit; 15th, Rahway, free permit; 16th, New Brunswick, free permit. Sunday evening, 17th, Bascom's drove into the yard. We were warned not to go to Princeton (college town). The students would destroy our house. " 'Tis natural to do that told not to do." On 18th arrived in Princeton. The college boys by hundreds surrounded us; they cheered, hooted and yelled. We had been surrounded by wolves, and, accustomed to Indians, so wife and I were calm, but determined to defend our house against marauders and relic-getters. Between waves of wild yells I told them we demanded civil treatment and would allow no barbarism, and if they intruded upon our rights I would shoot the intruder; but if treated civilly we were agreeable and easy to get along with. They settled; the worst ones retired; the young gentlemen bought books; we conversed with the professors; all treated us kindly after the first attack. The people in town said they never saw the students act so well with any traveler as with us. We expect to visit them again.

Mrs. Lasley " Tells Her Experience."

Thinking it would be interesting to the reader, I (the wife of the author of this book and the proprietor of the HOUSE ON WHEELS) have concluded to express my ideas of traveling. When I was quite a little girl I used to think and say, "Some day I will travel, if I am fortunate enough to have a husband."

I used to stand in front of the mirror and say, "Oh, dear, nobody will ever marry me, for I am so homely," but I learned that looks do not always count, and that dress does not make the man or the woman, for I was married before I was yet sixteen and have not regretted it. After marrying I commenced to think and plan how we could travel. I said, "Some day we will." We first did farming near Greeley, Colo. I helped my husband in the field. I learned to drive a team, to ride and plow, to cultivate the crops, &c., while my husband did the irrigating and ditching. We bought a team, plows, wagon, seed and harvesters on time, and got them all paid for except the harvester. In the Fall a note came due. The agent closed upon us, and our season's labor was swept away to pay and settle. My husband then got a Winter school at good price. In the Spring we located in Ft. Collins, Colo., and opened a shop. We did well, got us a house lot and commenced to make us a home.

In 1887 my health gave way. Our doctor said I could not live thirty days longer unless I was taken out into the open air. My husband disposed of his business and got an outfit (see pages 27 and 28 of this book).

How delighted I was; now I would see some of the world at least. Having started, we kept on and on until we reached Washington Territory (as it was then). By the way, my folks were all there, and they acted as a magnet for me at least. After having many hardships, my health was perfectly restored; my desire for travel had started into a flame; I believe I am a born traveler. I contented myself in Port Angeles for nearly five years, only taking one trip over east of the mountains during that time. One day my husband said he was going to California alone. Think of it! Leave his family to shift for themselves. I said: "Never will I consent for you to go alone. You gave up your business for my benefit; now I will go along, and together we will face the world as it comes." My husband had poor health; we had no money; our outlook was blue, so blue it was turning black. My husband asked for my idea of how we could all go along. I laid the plan of the Lasley Traveling Palace (known as the HOUSE ON WHEELS). You, reader, know how hard it was for my husband to be convinced that my idea of travel could be carried out. Finally all objections being met, we (my husband and I) went into the forest with axes, saws, sledge, wedges and frowe. He selected a fine large white cedar tree, and we chopped and sawed, it seemed to me, for about three hours until finally, crack! and there it goes, and the once giant of the forest lay at our feet as a conquered foe. That was only the beginning, for the tree had to be converted into shakes and lumber for our HOUSE

ON WHEELS.

We sawed out a chunk, split it into bolts; then rived it into material for our house, carried it to our lot, and there my husband made our house on wheels. I helped some in its construction. It finally being ready to move into, my heart almost failed me. When we commenced to move into it, so many things I thought I must have and no room to put them, but I sorted them, then sorted again and again, until finally I adapted my wants to the room. I must admit I felt rather cramped for room for a week or two until I got used to things. How little we realized what we had made or what we had undertaken. I did not then know we had made something that the people would care to look at and run after to see. My folks told us we were foolish; friends said we would soon be back. Others said we could never get far with "that thing." We said we did not know as we could, but we could try. Many an eye was moist when we bid our friends a last farewell and started on a long trip. The roads in Washington are almost impassable in the Spring and hard to travel over. I was lighthearted because I was realizing my long hope—traveling. We ran out of money, could get no work; we suffered for food; in places we could not get even water to drink. We met with people that snubbed us; still I did not despair. I said to myself, "I must brace up, for it was I that had planned this way to travel." I tried to brace up, but pen can never half express what we endured. You may say, "Why did you not stop in some nice town?" We could not; nothing to stop for; people living in the towns were, if anything, worse off than we were. We went forward, guided by an unseen Hand, whither we knew not.

.... TRAPED IN MY OWN CAGE: ....

In every town people came running to see the curious looking wagon, as they called it. Imagine how I felt—never had I been used to face any number of people to talk to them, try to entertain them or to answer their questions. I thought them impudent. Our business? Where going? Where from? How far? How long? How many of us? Why? When going to stop? When going away? Do you tell fortunes? Are you gypsies? Who are you? Have you any money? How do you make a living? are a few of the many questions asked us by all the callers, both old and young, great and small. At first I closed the door in their faces; that only excited their curiosity, and they went for the windows. I finally submitted to be looked at and be questioned until now I can cook our meals or attend to my home duties with a thousand looking at me and not worry me a bit.

The largest audience we had was in San Francisco.

The people came by thousands. We got newspaper notoriety owing to our mode of travel. We had traveled 1,200 miles. My desire to travel more was greater than ever; I desired to travel East. My husband had many fears as to us getting far upon the road. I said: "We have come 1,200 miles; we can go further." In June, 1895, we started again. Every day a few miles, slow but sure; but what of that; we were traveling, seeing the world; that was my fond desire. We again had many hardships. Sometimes for days we saw no one but foreigners, and they were looking after the railroad track. They refused us water; miles and miles of nothing to see but sage and rabbit brush, soap weed and cacti. Our eyes became tired of the monotony. "Look yonder!" we exclaim. "See!" the beautiful forest and shining lake of sparkling water. How we longed for the refreshing shade and a boat ride on the lake. Impatient to reach the place, we hurry up our horses, when, lo! we are doomed to disappointment. Looking again in a few minutes the forest and lake had disappeared, and only sage and alkali bottoms were in sight. Mountains, forests, cities, lakes and rivers have appeared to our views as plain as ever the real ones ever did, only to dissolve again, to our disgust.

This mirage is deceiving. It has lured many poor traveler beyond his ability to return, and their bones were found where, exhausted, they had died. We press forward, for go we must; to stop meant certain death. On and on, ten, twenty, thirty or more miles per day—same to see (just nothing). But look! Are we sure of our sight? Yes, yes. Away in the distance we could see the Rocky Mountains, their snow-capped peaks looming up. As we came nearer, how grand those lofty peaks, standing as silent judges over those lesser ones around them. But when we began to ascend them, to us they had lost their beauty, though still grand in size. We had crossed many mountains before the Rockies, but these were most difficult. Our team and ourselves were all tired out. The mountains in places are twelve miles up the sides of them; they are about the same down. Up, down, then repeat again and again, until from the top of one of the foothills we saw the fine city of Denver, Col.

I fancy I hear you, reader, say: "Oh, the beautiful scenery you have enjoyed!" Yes, we have seen some of the grandest scenery the mind could conceive of. If we could get wealth from scenery we would be very rich indeed; but we become tired of looking at even grand things. Just to think! We have been up in the air two and one-fourth miles high, the clouds way below us in the valleys. We have gathered flowers with one hand and put the other hand in banks of snow; snowballed each other in July. I was heartily sorry many a time I had ever started, but I wisely kept it to myself.

You see how determined we were to succeed. Nearly everybody said "You can't get to New York with that thing; it will fall to pieces before you go ten miles further."

☞ SOME NERVE TESTERS.

It took more than ordinary perseverance, with constant care, keeping in good humor and being full of hope. We did succeed beyond measure. You may say you would have thought that we would have found some place that would have suited our fancy, and we would have said this is good enough for us, and would have stopped, but I was determined to visit the City of New York, besides the intervening ones. Although it took us over two years to travel from San Francisco to New York, I am heartily glad I made the trip. It is rich in experience. From Denver to New York is a long, hard, lonely road to travel; but it is fine and pleasant as compared with some of the first of the road. At times we suffered from the heat and for the want of water. Some of the water in Texas was so foul our horses and dog refused to drink it. We had to strain it to use it at all. We learned to drink any kind of water that we could swallow. We were slowly traveling over one of the mesas, our team as well as ourselves nearly famished for water. Water, water, was all we desired. Suddenly we saw a man coming toward us (upon the road). We thought surely we would soon come to a ranch and get water. When we met we asked if he could tell us where we could find water. He asked us the same question. We answered him. He said: "About fifteen miles ahead you will come to an old sheep ranch. There is an old well there. If you have a rope you can draw enough out for a drink around." We thanked him, but our hearts almost failed us. It was now high noon. We renewed our courage and pushed forward. We passed through a field of ripe unharvested wheat. We let our horses eat it, also rubbed some in our hands and ate it. It alleviated our thirst a little. Still we craved water. Toward evening we came to the place; gathered all the rope we had (the well was seventy-five feet deep); with a small bucket we could get about a pint at a time. We all drank, and drank, a little at a time. We gave some to our team and dog; until, when all thirst was satisfied, we took a look at the water. It was rather muddy-like. When, horrors! it was literally filled with water lice and remains of dead mice. Say, reader, were you ever real thirsty in your life? That was but one of many experiences we have had to undergo. The children and myself have stayed alone until near midnight, while my husband, with the team and our dog, went down into some canyon in search of water. They, starting before dark, always succeeded. But, oh my! under what risk. The children would go to sleep; then I was alone; no, not alone either, for, listen, hear those sounds—'tis the howling of approaching wolves. Hear them all around; there must be a dozen or more. They make the cold chills run over me for the safety of myself and children. I have no fear for my husband; he has the dog; and wolves, unless they are very hungry, will not bother where there is a dog. I plucked up courage, went to the brink of the mountain and halloed as loud as I could, and listened for an answer. There was not a sound but the howling of those wolves. I returned and waited; then tried again. Finally, away in the distance I heard a faint far-away answer. It was a welcome sound, and ere long my careworn husband is again with his loving family. He has a couple of gallons of water he has carried about six miles.

But our journey has not been all unpleasant by any means. Many pleasant memories we retain of friends we have made and beautiful and pleasing things we have seen. We recall the visit of my husband's sister and her family to see us when in 'Frisco. We enjoyed their good company so much. We persuaded them to remain in 'Frisco, and she writes us they are pleased with their choice. My husband's brother visited us when near Denver. This we greatly appreciated; but my husband's moneyed sister (land poor) did not favor our mode of travel, and a chill we felt while in her company. In every state we have met very fine people indeed, and some just the reverse. Many times we have been invited into strangers' houses and been elegantly entertained, some few times for two or three days at a time. We felt more than thankful for their kindnesses.

OUR EXPERIENCE WITH A STRANGE WOMAN.

We were in northern Indiana in the month of March. The towns are few and far apart and the roads had been muddy, now frozen; travel slow. My husband had tried to get accommodation of the farmers for shelter for our team, but as usual the farmers all said "No room; am sorry; go to next neighbor." The sun was getting low, when I said: "Let Viola try; maybe they won't refuse a child." We came to a large, finely fitted place. "Go in, Viola, and try for shelter for our faithful horses." Rap, rap. "Who's there? What do you want?" we heard. "Are any of you sick? Are you in distress? Are you lousy? Are you honest? Can you all read?" These questions being answered to her satisfaction, she said: "I'll see." She slipped on her wraps and she and her husband came out to look us over. They counselled. Said he: "Take your horses and put them under the shed. There is hay in the mow and corn in the barn. Help yourself." So saying, they both returned to the house. "Viola, please go ask the woman to sell us a loaf of bread for supper." Said she: "No, I won't sell you any bread." I was preparing to make some hot cakes or biscuits and arranging for our meal. Looking out we saw the woman approaching (to give us a lecture, we supposed). Said she, in a rough voice: "You can't have any bread, milk nor anything else." I said: "Thank you." "I want you all to come into my house to supper." I protested. She insisted. "Just as you are, come along, right now." Fearing to refuse, we went. Oh, the style. On entering her house her tone changed. She was an angel in disguise. Her table was loaded with ham, eggs, potatoes, rice, onions, tea, coffee, bread, butter, pie, cake, fruits. The house was nicely carpeted and thoroughly warmed—a perfect home. Said she: "Make yourselves at home. Children, romp all you please and enjoy yourselves." They had two of their own. I helped her wash up the supper dishes. My husband chatted with her man. Nearing bedtime, we said we would go out to our house. "No," said she, "I have night suits, etc. You are all going to stay in here over night." She said that was her religion. We submitted. Oh, such nice beds! Their hands looked after the horses, and another day and night she detained us within her walls and insisted upon us stopping longer. We learned to love her for her kindness. Her memory we cherish. Their name is Webster. Treatment like that is Christian.

When we drove into the City of Greater New York how our hearts leaped for joy. We had succeeded in doing something nobody had ever accomplished—crossed America in a House on Wheels.

After arriving we were like a cat in a strange house. We were all over the city in no time, dodging here, there and everywhere, seeing the sights, like a panorama. I desire to state here that New York people are fine to sell books to. In fact, every city we visited (where the people are intelligent) we sold our books in great numbers; more so in the East than out West. We find the Eastern people very clever. The officers in most of the places are very obliging, allowing us to stop with our house on wheels upon the streets and stay as long as we desired and sell all the books we could. Especially kind in Washington, D. C.; Chester, Philadelphia, New York, Bridgeport, Providence, Newport, Taunton, Beverly, Portsmouth, Albany, Buffalo, Little Washington, Wheeling, Columbus, Cincinnati, St. Louis and San Francisco. We have had some novel experiences with the wearers of blue coats with brass buttons. Some of them delight to show their authority, but we were generally equal to the occasion.

AN IMPUDENT OFFICER.

In the beautiful city of Bridgeport we had stopped on one of the streets. My husband had gone in search of a stable with a yard attached, when suddenly I heard a gruff voice say: "Where is the owner of this outfit?" I said: "Gone out on business." Said he: "When did you water this team last?" I answered: "Just as we drove into this city." "I don't believe it," said he. I said: "You don't have to believe it." Said he: "I don't believe you have watered or fed this team for a week." I told him he was a fool for want of sense. The idea of us not caring for our team. "If you are so much interested in other people's business you can go buy a sack of oats and feed the team, if you wish to," I said. As to the team being thirsty, he was judging them by himself. He was partially angry and partially amused at my talk back to him. A bystander suggested I ask him how about that old, blind, stringhalted, spavined, half-starved horse he used to drive before he was elected inspector. I did so, but he made no answer. I asked him to show his badge. He said he had forgotten to put it on. When my husband came he tried his bark upon him, but my husband laughed at him and told him he would take care of our team without any of his help. He finally took his leave, having met his equal for once. He returned and bought a book of me, saying he bought it because I had defended our cause so nobly. I expect we will meet him again this Summer. If so I will sell him the book that this is in.

We have had several like experiences; but it takes all kinds of things and people to make up our experience. After having rough, hard times, to succeed in some places, we know how to appreciate the better and finer things of life. Kind reader, I will leave you to judge for yourself whether I enjoy traveling. I answer you, 'tis my choice to see the world.

We will travel another season in America. Then, if all is well, go over to Europe, and to Paris in time for the exposition. Home again, we expect to settle some place in the West. Now, dear reader, if you have not seen our little House on Wheels it will more than pay you to come and see a genuine curiosity, thoroughly original with us. We lead, others may follow. Financially we were at the foot of the ladder. Now we are steadily climbing upward. Some day we will have a stationary home; but we will see the world first. Who is it but says: "When I get money I am going to see the world." We are enjoying the sights of the world and making a good living at the same time. Please don't misjudge us—come and see for yourself. We are known as the happy family. If you are skeptical as to us having made this trip, come, examine our credentials and your doubts will fly away.

MY HUSBAND.

Most wives will end their story with:
  "Ah, well, men are but human."
I long to tell the secret of
  A truly happy woman.

Through all the sunshine-lighted years,
  Lived now in retrospection,
My husband's word brought never tears,
  Nor caused a sad reflection.

Whate'er the burdens of the day,
  Unflinching, calm and steady,
To bear his part—the larger half—
  I always find him ready.

House-cleaning season brings no frown,
  No sarcasm, pointed keenly;
Through carpets up, and tacks head down
  He makes his way serenely.

Our evenings pass in converse sweet,
  Or quiet contemplation.
We never disagree, except
  To "keep up conversation."

And dewy morn of radiant June,
  Fair moonlight of September,
April with bird and brook atune,
  Stern, pitiless December—

Each seems to my adoring eyes
  Some new grace to discover.
For he, unchanging through the years,
  Is still my tender lover.

Adieu, dear reader.

MRS. MARY L. LASLEY.
Queen of the Traveling Palace.

(Our Card.)

```
*―――――――――――――――――――――――*
| M. E. A. LASLEY.      MARY L. LASLEY. |
|                                       |
|           KING AND QUEEN              |
|                OF                     |
|     THE ONLY HOUSE ON WHEELS,         |
|                OR                     |
|      LASLEY'S TRAVELING PALACE.       |
|                                       |
|       JOURNEY AROUND THE WORLD.       |
*―――――――――――――――――――――――*
```

(☞ THE KING NOW TALKS AGAIN :)
A BARBAROUS RECEPTION.

April 20th B's and us drove on to the streets of Trenton, at the Monument. We learned the business center was seven or eight blocks away, so he and I went down to get a central stable and yard; some trouble to find; got location in U. S. Hotel yard. Returning, we found his house, but mine gone, no one knew where. Inquired of patrolman. He said he had driven an outfit off the street. I asked "why he had not moved the other one, too." Said "there was no crowd around the other one." I asked if any of my family was selling books. Said "No." "Why did you move them?" " 'Cause I wanted to." "Where are they?" Said he: "Don't know and don't care." I respect an officer, but not such a thing as that. Some boys came running up; said they could find my house on wheels for me. Gladly I followed down the avenue, turned into a street, then into an alley, finally into a lot in the rear of a saloon. I greeted my family and asked how they came to be there. Wife said a policeman had moved them three times. saying "if she did not leave the highways he would pull the outfit." Finally this woman offered this enclosed lot free. My wife gave two books and pictures to the woman for her kindness. On going out of the lot a man demanded 50 cents rent. I told him to get it, and drove out. After arriving at the hotel yard I went for a street permit. Failed. Reported the police action to the chief. Said he: "I presume the officer did just right." I told him New York people spoke of them as foreigners, and they impressed it upon us. We had never been treated as rudely over 6,000 miles of travel. Trenton's police are the most rude of any met with. At

Bristol free permit; sold 120 books; fine people; fine officers.

    (Newspaper Clippings, Headlines.)
"A House Wagon."
    "Built for Travel Across the Continent." "From Pt. Angles, Washington."
"Large Crowds Gather to See Lasley's 'House on Wheels' at U. S. Hotel."
    —Daily True American,
    Trenton, N. J., April 23, 1898.

April 22: Philadelphia. Police extra kind. They got us good location, corner Frankford and Hart lane. We saw City Clerk, Mayor and Chief of Police. They seemed surprised at me asking for a permit. "Why, brother, thee dost not need a permit at all to sell literature upon our streets; go ahead, sell all you can; don't stay too long in one place to cause a jam. Good day. Success." Central lot location; hard to get; so from Snider avenue and Seventeenth street we worked the south side of the city. We visited Navy Yard; Government officers showed kindness. We got relics and souvenirs from battleships; visited the Mint, City Hall, etc. Fine city; clever people. We sold our books in the city until May 9th, then south again. Free permit at Wilmington; lot of books sold; officers clever.

CLOSE CALL.

On going over one of the hills of Delaware we encountered a storm. Oh, how the lightning flashed! It blinded us. We could hear **it swizz** as it cut the air; the heavens burned with **the heat;** the horses stopped and reeled, our brains seemed to be on fire. Three times **the** lightning struck within less than fifty **feet of us.** Following the electric display the rain descended **in torrents,** flooding the road and washing great gullies on the hillside. After passing from around us the storm abated.

Our house does not leak, so we care but little about a rainstorm. After crossing the (seemingly deserted) hills of western Delaware we arrived in Baltimore on May 16th.

MY DARING ACT BRINGS REWARD.

Stopped our house at a corner. I went to look for a stable. I found one, but it was a high-toned coach stable, fine office, etc. They had no room, did not know of any and did not care to be bothered. I thanked them. Turning to leave the office I saw there was a storm on hand, so remained indoors; it thundered and lightened; **the rain poured down,** the gutters soon filled with wild, rushing water, carrying debris of all kinds. It changed to hail; it pelted everything; some of the stones were an inch in diameter. Just then some one cried: "Just see! Yonder comes old Dave's team." With others I looked out. Sure enough, yonder came dashing up the street a runaway, the large horses dragging a wagon. Ahead of them stood a row of carriages, the occupants inside not knowing the danger coming. I looked to see who would risk their life to save the people. No one stirred. I knew my ability and courage. I quickly gauged the speed, out I flew, leaped as far as I could over the raging water (getting wet only to my thighs). Soon was alongside of the runaway; grasped the bridle and swinging to them I sheered them away from the carriages and by voice and pulling soon had them stopped. The proprietor and men at the stable were so much interested they ran out upon the walk into the storm to get a better view of my action. Soon the owner appeared, breathless. He thanked me kindly. I returned to the stable to await the storm's abatement. The proprietor was the first to speak. "I say, stranger, where is your House on Wheels? Go bring it around here. I'll find you a good place to stop; am sorry we have no place here for you; such a fine, daring act as that of yours deserves to be rewarded." Storm over, I found my house. They had been sheltered by a large building. I returned to the stable. "I say, Sam, saddle up that bay horse; go show this man the best way to the Hand hotel stable yard. I say! You make sure he gets there O. K. Keep him around on those smooth, best streets." "All right, sah," and a finely dressed colored man with a large umbrella proceeded to carry out his order. "I say, madame, we ought to have some of those books I see you have for sale; give us out here about a dozen. Only $1.25; that is good. Good by. Sam, go slow, be sure." The best streets in places were worse than in any city we ever traveled through. After about two miles of twisting about we were told by our guide we had arrived safely at the oldest hostelry in Baltimore; they knew of our coming, arrangements having been made by telephone. It was a good location, very central. We would probably never have found it but for the above recorded incident.

The city officials were dilatory in granting us a street permit; so after four days headed for Washington, D. C., at which place we arrived on Monday, May 23. Distance from New York, 245 miles by the road we came.

AT U. S. CAPITAL CITY.

Calling upon the district officers for **permit**, they kindly assured us no permit was necessary. "Just go any place; sell all the books you please." We put up at the Tyson hotel yard (another old hostelry of note). We met often and had pleasant chats with the owner of the place, Mr. Tyson. His family also called upon us. We stopped in front of the patent office, visited it, took views and sold books. We visited all the places of note, took views and sold our books. We were at the White House on a reception day; shook hands with our President, presented to him one of our books and photos; visited the Capitol, the Treasury by special permit (war rules), the Library, Smithsonian, Agricultural building, Washington's monument, the postoffice dead letter department, the Government cemetery and other places of note. We took our house every place we visited, and while part of us visited the places the balance of the family sold books to those gathered to see our curious house; then the other portion of our family visited and the first ones sold books. We never leave our house entirely alone (relic hunters too many). We had to guard it to keep it. If space would permit I would like to describe the places we visited, the things we saw, the beautiful large paintings at the Capitol, the beautiful grounds around the buildings, the statuary in the different places in the city, the things we saw at the National Museum, the description of the monument and how constructed, the stairway going up (we walked up); the views we got and the sensation of riding down in the elevator. Suffice it, we enjoyed all the things to be seen. We went to Mount Vernon, visited Washington's home, also his tomb, had a steamboat ride on the Potomac, then returned to Washington. The weather had become very hot and sultry; so on June 9 we headed northward, arriving again in Baltimore on Saturday, the 11th. Crossing through the city, in front of the Barnard Hotel, I broke down a wheel and the coupling; paid $1.50 to a truck to haul our house three or four squares. On Monday we had the repairs made; cost, $7.50. On Tuesday tried to cross the city again. On Baltimore street we broke the other front wheel tire; removed the wheel and took it to a shop to have it repaired. A crowd soon gathered; explanations of our position, and the family sold lots of books, till finally a patrolman came. He ordered my wife to leave the street. She said she was in her own home and was satisfied to stay where she was. He said: "If you don't move I'll pull you." "Well, if you desire, and you think you are able, you can pull me; but it may be a heavier task than you are used to. Please, Mr. Officer, look around," said my wife (with a twinkle in her eye). On going to the front and seeing but three wheels he thought, as the wife said, "he was not able to pull her," so decided to let it remain. He forbade her selling our books, but every time he turned his back she sold lots of them. Returning with the wheel, soon we were at rest at Eagle hotel yard.

TWO STRANGE CHARACTERS.

Soon after locating in the Eagle yard among those who came to see out outfit, buy our books, etc., were two certain young men. Said one: "I desire a kodak picture of your outfit, please, family and all." "Excuse us; we never sit for a picture; that curio we never allow. We have photos of our complete outfit, well finished, including the house, the family, the horses, our dog and our bird; these we sell; to give away kodak pictures of the same, we can't consider it," replied my wife.

"I'll pay you for your trouble," said he. "How much?"

"About 25 cents, I presume." "Yes." "Well, sir, your allowance is too small; if you had offered $5.00 to be permitted to take a picture of our outfit maybe then you might have impressed my mind as being a liberal kodak fiend, but, sir, you will never get a picture of our outfit at all. If you desire one of our photos, here they are, for only 10 cents," said the Queen of the Traveling Palace, fitting action to her words. She exhibited several photos of the outfit complete, also personal photos. These did not suit him. He acted gruffly and left, to look around the house. His companion looked very much amused at the conversation.

Said he: "I bought one of your books, and would like to more minutely examine your outfit. What, please, is this on this wheel?" "There comes my husband. Say, dear, here are some people; if you show them around the house perhaps they will buy some books." I said to them, if they cared they might make a tour around the house. The register; the construction of our house; the complication of the coupling; the map of our route; a large canvas painting; showed them we had our small wheels in the rear; showed a photograph taken of us when we were in San Francisco.

. The clippings from newspapers from Pt. Angeles, Wash., to last ones in their city; I explained the construction of the inside of our house; then introduced our book and pictures. They having been entertained, bought lots of books of me. The kodak man and his chum seemed well pleased. "Please give me one of those photos your wife spoke of," said his chum. I wrote our autograph with both my right and my left hand on the photo, claiming to be the champion right and left hand autograph writer. This interested him more than ever. He handed me 25 cents for it, saying "Keep the change." I thanked him. They departed. In the course of an hour he called again. "Have you some of those larger books? Please let me have three copies (35 cents each). I wish you well. Good day." He retired. Again he returned. "You have other photos, have you not?" "Yes." "Please let me have one of each. One, two, three, four; here is a dollar. They are worth it. The photos of noted travelers like you people can't be gotten every day. I desire them to place in my cabinet. Here is my card. Don't fail to write me.—Dr. Gilbert Smith, No. —, Baltimore. If you desire a physician while in the city I am at your service, free. Good day." I showed his card to my wife. "I could have told you he was a physician," said my wife. "The business of the kodak fiend?" "Why, he is a lawyer, of course," said she. Physicians treat us with more consideration than any other class of professional men. With pleasant memories revived by Dr. Smith's action we retired for the night, thankful our lot was as pleasant as it is. Our day's sale was $13.70. Next morning, the 15th, wife soon had breakfast over and I the team fed. Visitors began to arrive early, among them Dr. Smith. Said he: "I came early for fear you might have concluded to leave town. I desire to give you a little present. Come with me; won't take long." I followed. Into a fine grocery store. "Please put me up some staple groceries, such as a family can use; we will take them with us." Coffee, sugar, flour, bacon, prunes, rice, tea, etc. I called a halt. "Please don't break my outfit down; cost money for repairs." He smiled and said: "You can use them; they will come in handy." He hailed a passing car, saying, "We will return this way." We chatted about our country, of hunting, fishing, etc. He said he would enjoy traveling as we are, etc. At the car door he said: "Be good to yourself; good by." My wife was agreeably surprised upon opening the packages.

On the 16th just as we were leaving the yard up came our friend, Dr. Smith. "Here is a letter. You can use it." It read: "I have thoroughly investigated and have found that the Lasleys of the House on Wheels are just as they represent themselves to be—from the state of Washington—and I heartily recommend them to all intelligent people. The family is one of interest. I give them permission to use this recommendation as they see fit."—(Signed)   Gilbert Smith, M. D. "Be sure and write me. Don't forget to send me new photos. Good by. God bless you." With pleasant memories again we started north. On Tuesday, June 21, we arrived at Philadelphia. Having worked the city as we went south concluded to drive on through. At noon drove upon a vacant lot in Tioga to feed and get our dinner. Before dinner was over a large crowd had gathered and we had sold lots of books. One old lady, with tears in her eyes, said: "I have bought your books and photos. I have been reading about you in the papers. I have all your pictures and history I could get. I am so glad to have found you; seems like I have known you before. Please stay till to-morrow, so my family can come and see you all." I went to a livery stable adjoining and found them white people. Hay and stabling over night for our two horses only 37 cents—lowest price recorded east of Buffalo; average cost, $1.00 per night for hay only. We stayed. We lectured, our books sold well. Repeated day after day until the week wore away.

FEW NEWSPAPER HEADLINES.
"Across a Continent in a Large Wagon."
"The Lasley Family's Long Journey in Their House on Wheels.
"A Four Years' Ride; Two Children Have Been Born in the Conveyance—How They All Live."
"Philadelphia Inquirer," April 27, 1898.

LASLEY'S PARLOR CAR.
"The Only House on Wheels That Has Crossed the American Continent."
"The Republican," May 10, 1898.

"From Over Western Hills and Mountains A Unique Vehicle Came Into Baltimore Last Night, Its Occupants Having Had Many Strange Experiences En Route."
"The World," Baltimore, Md., May 17, 1898.

"LIFE IN HOME ON WHEELS.
"Lasley Family's Wonderful Experiences Within Four Years.—Rode 6,700 Miles for Health.
"Forded Rivers, Crossed Mountains, Sweltered in sun at 120, Froze in Snow at 18 Below Zero."
"Philadelphia Record," May 15, 1898.

After leaving Philadelphia we were soon at Princeton, June 28, town very quiet.

At Elizabeth the officers were kind, but not the mosquitoes.

At Jersey City took ferry for Brooklyn.

At Coney Island we procured a location at $25.00 per week; we sold books, bathed and with complimentary tickets enjoyed flying ponies, shoot the rapids, shoot the chutes, Ferris wheel, City of Cairo, the bikes, the ponies, scenic railroads, etc.

"There is but one Coney Island." After seeing the sights and enjoying the delightful ocean baths and cooling sea breezes we prepared for our summer northeast trip by repairing our house and refitting the wheels and other necessary repairs. We had again domiciled at Convent avenue and 150th street (Washington Heights stables), where the proprietor had said "You are welcome to return whenever you see fit," which we did, and as a business man he received us cordially. We had made many friends there and they were glad to see us return, shook our hands and said: "We welcome you back again."

"ACROSS THE CONTINENT."

"The Lasley Family Traveled in Their Own House."

"Evening Star," Washington, D. C., May 26, 1898.

"Home on Wheels Came 7,000 Miles, In It a Family Has Lived for More Than Four Years.

"To Make Tour of Europe.

"Came Over Brooklyn Bridge Into Manhattan Yesterday and Drew Big Crowd."

"The World," New York, July 20, 1898.

The following is one of many recommends given without being asked, showing we have been where we say we have, also showing what people think of us:

"Office of Hugh Reilly, New York, Dec. 13, 1897.

"This is to certify that Mr. M. E. A. Lasley, proprietor of the House on Wheels, has been my tenant from Dec. 6 to date. He has been honest and fair and has acted in a gentlemanly manner. Also his wife deserves great credit for keeping herself and family so neat and clean.

(Signed) "HUGH REILLY,

"Proprietor Merchants' Stables, 510 to 524 W. 14th street, New York."

On leaving Mr. Reilly said: "If you are in this part of the city again you are welcome to stop here again."

All liverymen have said the same.

Being again in readiness, we bade our new friends adieu. We drove over by Boston road to New Rochelle. The officers procured us a central lot location and were very clever. They gave us the privilege of selling our books on Sunday to any who desired to buy, of which there were many, and they all seemed to be church goers or comers.

July 25th, at Port Chester, we paid $1 for the privilege of selling our books on a private lot. The resident business men (when they heard me tell of it) insisted I go and demand it paid back. I objected, because the amount was so small. They insisted on me doing it, so I did so, but the city clerk said he had turned the money into the treasurer. So no pay for my trouble. It became noised about us being there and a very attentive audience gathered in the evening. We sold lots of books. Robert sang, then he took up his usual collection. He got $1.70, the largest collection he ever received for singing. Fine, clever people.

QUEER TERMINUS TO AN ACCIDENT.

"Let me ride your wheel a little bit, young man," said I to one of the visitors. "Will it hold me up?"

"Oh, yes." I mounted and had not ridden it five rods when down went the hind wheel. Examining it, I found it had been broken and repaired before. I returned his wheel to him and said: "You go get the rim repaired and I will help pay for it." He went to a shop, ordered a new wheel complete and said to present the bill to the proprietor of the House on Wheels, which they did. I refused to pay the bill ($3.60), but said I would pay half. His father became indignant. He went to a lawyer, then to a judge; had a case made out; had me brought (by a constable) before the judge. He stated his case. I stated my side. I offered again to pay half on the new wheel. He said: "I want all or none." The judge again asked him if he rejected half. He said he did. The judge said: "Lasley, you are dismissed. Mr. ——, you must pay the costs." I went on about our business (of selling our books). He bothered us no more, preferring "no loaf to half a one," and that a new one.

A CLEVER BUSINESS MAN!

At Stamford July 27. Free street permit on square; big crowds; big sale of book. While my wife was lecturing I was selling books. A nicely dressed man approached. Said he: "Here is my card. After you close business come to my place for supper." "Thanks," said I, "we will, with pleasure." At 9.30 p. m. we drove to his business place. Soon we were enjoying a repast fit for a regal king and queen.

(Obiter dictum of John H. Lee by Lasley.)

Oh, you noted people, whoever you may be,
Will surely be invited by this Silver Dollar Lee,
Be you sport or politician,
   No difference you will see,
You will all be dined and wined,
   By smart Silver Dollar Lee.
His place is one of beauty;
   You will easy see the sign;
If you look upon the marble floor,
   You'll think you've found a mine.
And don't you be misguided,
   For this Silver Dollar Lee
Has used the artist's, sculptor's
   And mechanic's skill, you'll see.
Of one thing this man prides to tell,
   He always serves his patrons well.
With elegance and grace their orders fill
With best of everything on bill.
When once you've gone, your song will ever be,
I stopped, when in Port Stamford, with Silver Dol-
    lar Lee.

MORE KINDNESS.

Norwalk, 28.—Free street permit. Said Mr. H. G. Hamilton, "That is my hotel over there. Mr. Lee, of Stamford, desires you to dine with us. Dinner is waiting."

Their dinner and service was fine. Toward evening a gentleman said to me: "My name is G. Fred Austin. I desire your family to eat supper at my place. I won't let neither Lee nor Hamilton be more courteous than I." We accepted. Oh, the fine supper, everything the market afforded.

I said to my wife, "The Yankees lead in cleverness."

At Bridgeport, 29.—Free street permit, but poor location, Wall and Water streets.

New Haven, 30.—No permit obtainable, although citizens said, "others were allowed upon the streets."

"7,000 Miles on Wheels."
"Family of Seven Who Make Their Home in a Wagon,
"Reached This City Yesterday.
"Journey for Health and Pleasure from Seattle; Have Been Everywhere."
  "New Haven Register," July 31, 1898.

Meriden, Aug. 6.—Free permit, good location, clever officers.

"Traveling Palace."
"House on Wheels Anchors in This City To-Day."
"Daily Journal," Meriden, Conn., Aug. 6, 1898.

HARSH TREATMENT.

At Hartford, 8.—No permit obtainable.

My wife and I had been down into the city and bought her a new bicycle. When we returned there was a crowd. We offered and sold few books. Soon a policeman came into the lot of the livery. Said he:

"All you people not belonging here will have to get out;" then he stood at the gate permitting no one to enter unless they had business with the livery. Being handicapped, we concluded not to pay out any more money there so pulled out to find more congenial people.

Springfield, Mass.—The officers were very kind; they treated us like we were human beings. The sour makes the sweet taste sweeter.

"A Home on Wheels.
"Nomadic Life of a Family Which Arrived in Town Yesterday."
"Springfield Republican," Aug. 10, 1898.

At Worcester, Aug. 13.—At Hildreth's livery The Spy interviewed us, gave us fine, long, good, kind article. The Spy is a nice, clean paper. The people are fine book buyers.

"On Wheels—Strange House Appears."
"HAPPY FAMILY
"Is Aboard and Has Traveled Four Years."
"The Worcester Spy," Aug. 14, 1898.

A CHANGED PROGRAMME.

At South Framingham, Aug. 16.
We had planned to store our outfit in Boston, then riding bicycles to 'Frisco as a family, then return for our European tour. My wife had bought her a wheel

in Hartford and immediately learned to ride it. We got Leona a wheel at South Framingham (she learned to ride it in less than two hours).

Viola and I had ridden from Western New York. Afterward I persuaded my wife to give up the trip for the present. She says she is going to ride a wheel yet across America. I presume she will.

At Boston, Aug. 20.—Our experience in that city is not pleasant to remember. The officers tried to be clever, but there was so much red tape and so much cross sword of cliques that henchmen and principals were afraid of each other. There was more rudeness of speech than any other city we ever traveled in, even the motormen and conductors and nicely dressed women were in the habit of hallooing at persons differing in looks from Boston people. We were glad when we left the narrow, rough, crooked, crowded streets of Boston, with its loud mouthed people, behind us. In proportion to the people, we sold less books in Boston and paid higher prices for things we bought, than in any city we had been in. We have lost no love for Boston.

Reception at Lynn, Aug. 26.—Got good central lot, opposite depot. The papers gave us illustrated write-ups. We had thousands of visitors and we sold lots of books to them. Many kind words and good wishes were spoken. Stayed in Lynn for a week.

At Beverly, Sept. 2.—Free location, side of city hall. Sold lots of books.

At Salem Willows, Sept. 5.—(Labor Day). Was a hit for us; heaviest book sale made in New England up to this time.

Portsmouth, N. H., Sept. 8.—Free permit; large sales.

At Rochester Fair, Sept. 12.—Paid $10 for location. Fair no good for us. Weather frosty.

SOUTHWARD.

Through Exeter, Newton, At Haverhill, Sept. 19.—No permit, poor location on lot; few books.

Lawrence, 22.—Free permit; good location. Sold lots of books; clever people.

Lowell, Sept. 24.—No permit; officers snobbish. Children very rude; few books

At Arlington, 28.—Fine people; clever officers. Sold lots of books.

Cambridge no good.

Quincy, 30.—No permit; good lot free; clever people; few books.

At Brockton Fair, Oct. 3.—Location, $15; rain, rain. Wednesday and Thursday clear; immense crowds. Red letter day for us, Thursday; sold double number of books of Labor Day. Dinner with Big Infant, of Western fame. Fine people, but very skeptical.

At Taunton.—Free street. Papers gave us big puff. Lots of books; very clever people.

Fall River no good.

At Newport, Oct. 15.—Free permit; fine resort. Nice people and officers. On 18th tried Fall River again; paid $1 for street permit; no good.

At Providence, R. I.—Free permit; fine location. Book, book, book their cry. In eight days sold over 1,400 of them. Extra nice people; no rudeness; well behaved. Got material; built us another house (on gears of wagon); got another horse; forward again.

Nov. 21 at New London.—People skeptical; few books. On 24th had fine turkey dinner; 25th our annex got on fire, damage $15.

At New Haven, 26.—Snow storm stayed us; applied for snow hauling; refused because I was not a resident.

PRESS HEADLINES.

"The Lasleys in Distress."

"Family in House on Wheels stalled in Orange street. Couldn't get work in New Haven. Mayor Farnsworth declined to help out travelers from the Pacific coast, so are compelled to remain until the roads are passable.—Mr. Lasley and fine arts."

New Haven "Register," Dec. 4, 1898.

THE BEGGARS OF 'FRISCO.

For the first few days after arriving in 'Frisco starvation was close to our door. We were too proud to let our condition be known, except to a few, as recorded (pages 71 and 72 of this book); the anguish was terrible until the change, as told on page 75 (this book); then we felt rich. We offered to feed any hungry person; many accepted, but none of them seemed to be as hungry as we had been. Most of them asked for money to eat on. I said money to drink on, you mean. Asking them to eat with us, their stomach gave the lie to their tongue. There was a fine eating place near by where a person could get all they could eat of good, nice, clean grub (Western term for edibles) for 10 cents. For 30 cents we could get more than my family desired to eat. Before going to our meals I would say: "Now, if there is any poor, hungry person here, come go and get a good free meal." One day I noticed a one-legged, young, poorly-clad beggar in the crowd. As usual, I put the same request. It struck him. "I'll go." "You are welcome," said I. I had him eat at our table. I tried to find out his history, experience, etc. He would not carry on any conversation. He wanted to know if I was not a reporter in disguise. Assuring him I was not and was just a common traveler, he became more congenial. I tried to persuade him to eat enough to satisfy a hungry man, as he had said he was, but I failed. He ate but little, finished, excused himself and tried to leave. I retained him till we were done. After paying the bill I said to the cashier: "Any time this poor cripple desires a meal, let him have it. When we come for our meal I will pay his. He stepped out ahead of us, but I noticed he did not hurry away, but sidled toward a door and beckoned for me to come. I slipped to his side, wondering what he now wanted.

Said he: "I am here to find out the truth. It has been reported to me that you offer to feed any poor person, and I came to try you. I am satisfied it is so. I want to tell you something. We beggars are organized and have a strong society, with money to our credit in the bank. I am the treasurer. You, sir, will never again be asked to give a beggar anything. You will know by their action after to-night. Good by." He was gone. We record the fact.
that never again were we asked for money, or anything to eat while we were in the State of California.

Bridgeport, Dec. 7.—Rested two days. Stamford, Dec. 10; New Rochelle, 13; Williams Bridge, 14; East 117th street, Dec. 22. Free street permit. Sold our books at corner Third avenue and 125th street from our house. Fine people; clever officers. Sold lots of books.

PAPER HEADLINES.

"The House on Wheels" at 531 East 117th street.

"The Hon. M. E. A. Lasley, author, traveler and proprietor, may look like a 'durned fool,' but he has hit on 'how to get rich.'

"Maybe he has as much brains as whiskers."

The New York "Press," Jan. 14, 1899.

KIND NEIGHBORS.

Our location was well chosen; neighbors soon called upon us, and asked us to call upon them. Among those whose friendship proved most sincere were J. G. Wilson and family, of 526 East 117th street; H. Markle and family. We spent many pleasant evenings with them, and partook of their hospitality. They offered to care for us during the raging blizzard, but being comfortable in our little houses, we thanked them and remained cosey and warm within at our quarters.

Thus ends our book, "Across America in the Only House on Wheels." We have not (for want of space) gone into detail in things we would like to, but this is for the people, a cheap book for the masses. It shows how a poor but ambitious family can turn disaster into benefit, and be healthy, have a good living, enjoy life, see all, and be happy. Reader, you may expect other publications, especially "Pioneer Life in the West; or, The Boy From a Buckeye Town." Inquire for it at dealers.

Come and see our house. Buy our photos, especially the photo of our boy singer, little Robert. Agents for this book wanted; terms liberal. Address, with stamp for terms,

M. E. A. LASLEY,
Author and Proprietor of Lasley's Traveling Palace.
Address: General Delivery, New York City, N. Y.

AN OMISSION.

Reading our book collectively, I find I have shown partiality, so this is added to even up.

EXTRA CLEVER TREATMENT.

After arriving at Wappinger Falls, N. Y., we came to a temporary halt in front of Sweet, Orr & Co.'s overalls and pants factory. Soon among others came a gentleman who proved to be Mr. Goring, superintendent of the factory. Said he, "Would not you like to visit and inspect our factory? We are the biggest overall manufacturers in the world." I said, "With pleasure." I was especially interested in their corduroy suits, and asked how they were made, as I had worn many overalls of their make and not a pair ever ripped. There are more of Sweet, Orr & Co.'s overalls, pantaloons and corduroy worn out West than all other makes put together. They give best satisfaction; command the best price. This statement from me pleased the superintendent amazingly. On passing through the cutting room, he ordered my measure taken, also measured Robert (our only boy). On returning to the office he asked our boy to remember his name, so told him and us of a teacher by name of Goring who had a pupil who could not remember her name, so she said, "If you desired to enter a large house, how would you get the door open?" "Why, I would go ring the bell," answered the child. Said the teacher, "My name is Goring." After that the child remembered her as Go ring the bell. In coming out of the factory he handed me a package and said, "I hope they will fit. Wear them; remember the giver." As a compliment, I placed Sweet, Orr & Co.'s advertising card upon our house, and it was there when we drove into Newburg, N. Y., Sept. 30th, '97, their home factory location.

A NEW SURPRISE.

We had secured a street permit and there was a big crowd around us, books selling fast. A man with quick step came up, asked me how I came to have that ad. upon there. I told him of our treatment by Sweet, Orr & Co.'s superintendent, and that was a compliment to them. Said he, "Give me a dollar's worth of books, photos; well, yes, I'll take two dollars' worth of these fine photos of your outfit. Good-day." And he was gone. Soon after a fine looking young man came up; said he, "We have heard of others. To-morrow you and family please call at our home factory of Sweet, Orr & Co." We did. We were kindly received by the superintendent, Mr. C. W. Bartrum, and foreman. Myself and boy were the recipients of another pair of corduroy pants. I have worn mine every day since, and not a hole or a break in them. They said, "They will never rip." "Oh," said I, "I know that, for I have always chosen your goods out West; gave me best satisfaction."

If any of the firm of Sweet, Orr & Co. sees this, I wish to congratulate you as makers of the best corduroy and overalls ever used by man. I admire your button and band fasteners, also. As these are the only factories we have ever been allowed to visit, we feel more pleased at our reception. Other factories have said, "No, your notoriety would cause all hands to stop and look at you, and that means loss." Although when we were conducted through their sewing room 500 operators stopped and looked at least a minute each, making a loss of over eight hours, not one word of complaint was heard. The hands seemed satisfied, and said their success was also due to their kind treatment by the firm. Dealers in the goods say the firm is honest and square dealers.

We wish you all of your well-earned success.

Yours, M. E. A. LASLEY,

Laborer, traveler, author and proprietor of the only House on Wheels.

www.ingramcontent.com/pod-product-compliance
Lightning Source LLC
Chambersburg PA
CBHW030301170426
43202CB00009B/835